Dear Irene and
    Mike: How wonderful to be the
birth you and share the
joy of your marriage, your love,
and, let us not forget Mike, you're our
mentorship and friendship with Julie, our
daughters! Let us spend loads of time together
here in NY and - hey! Come to JtoS -
                                    With love,
                                    Joan
                                    May 13, 2008

Virgin Gorda

An Intimate Portrait

Virgin Gorda
An Intimate Portrait

Painting at the Watersports Building, Little Dix Bay.

photographs and text
by
Joan Massel Soncini, Ph.D.

Other Titles by
VIRGIN ISLAND BOOKS

The Drinking Man's Guide to the BVI

Sunfun Calypso

The Virgins' Treasure Isle

The Baths

A to Z of the Sea

Printed in China

All photographs © Joan Massel Soncini
except on pages 32, 33, 44, 45, 52, 55, 66, 67.

ISBN 978-0-9667923-5-5

Layout by Julia Donovan of Graphic Design (BVI) Ltd.

Published by Virgin Island Books

Contents

VI   Virgin Gorda

Dedication

For the people who participated in making this book a reality, both those who helped me
get to those people, Julia Leonard and Dr. Esmeralda O'Neal, and the actual people I interviewed.

Thank you Julia Donovan, for putting the book together with your marvelous graphic art and style; Ralph O'Neal, for serving as a sort of "Greek Chorus", coming into and out of the book with your special perspectives and wisdom; Esther Wheatley, for your spirituality; Rebecca Leung and Tony Silard, for beautiful, caring editing; Richard Lenert, for transcribing the original tapes – was

that ever challenging! Lesley Ehlers, for the original "Dummy Book", which gave me what became the book's cover and form; Mario, my beloved husband, always standing so close by my side; Tony, Julie, Danny, Marc and Justine, my children, son-in-law and granddaughter, of whom I am so very proud!

Joan Massel Soncini, Ph.D.

Foreword
by the Honorable Ralph T. O'Neal

It is a great pleasure for me to write the foreword to this important book, in particular due to my own devotion to the people of Virgin Gorda. This is not only a beautiful photography book, but much more importantly a spoken history told by the some thirty people interviewed by the author.

Having fifteen years on Virgin Gorda, in which she has made so many close friendships, Joan Massel Soncini, Ph.D., decided to use her many talents and devote herself to creating this book. A psychotherapist and adjunct professor at the New York University, specializing in cross-cultural issues, Joan is also an accomplished photographer. She has had many one-person, major photography shows in Italy, her husband Mario's native country. In this book, Joan strives to let us tell our *own* story, namely how Virgin Gorda has evolved over the last century, with special attention to Little Dix Bay, which opened in 1964, launching us from a peasant society into a commercial-industrial society.

In the following pages you will hear the voices of both

right: Frangipani;
below right:
Gift shop at the Bitter End Yacht Club.

people born and raised in Virgin Gorda, as well as those who have come to live and work on the island. Each person interviewed adds his or her own special perspective on some aspect of our island: cultural life during the early years in the Valley and North Sound; advances in education, hotels and restaurants, activities and entertainment, etc.; concerns about the effects of change; and, finally, a deep appreciation and love for this island and her inhabitants.

Enjoy!

clockwise from top left: Goats roam along the roads; Puck, owner of the Flying Iguana bar; Poolside at the Bitter End; Red berries on a palm tree; above right: Sunset above Pond Bay.

Introduction to
Virgin Gorda: An Intimate Portrait

Welcome to Virgin Gorda, the easternmost island of the British Virgin Islands. In 1493 Christopher Columbus noted the island's long, narrow shape and what appeared to be a round belly. Thus he affectionately named her the 'Fat Virgin.'

People call the 50 islands which make up the British Virgin Islands a variety of names, including 'The Land That Time Forgot,' 'Nature's Little Secrets' and 'Paradise.' Adjectives such as 'gorgeous,' 'stunning,' 'tranquil' and extraordinary also come to mind as you admire the glorious landscape of Virgin Gorda.

At first glance, this book looks like a coffee table book with beautiful photographs. However, there is so much more to Virgin Gorda. You will experience this island in the wonderful stories of her inhabitants, both natives and newcomers, who share their experiences in Virgin Gorda and discuss her transformation over the years.

From my first interviews with ninety-year-old Waldo O'Neal to his younger brother, the Honorable Ralph T.

O'Neal, to later interviews with Shereen Flax-Charles, the "Calypso Monarch" singer who works for BVI Tourism, and Gracia Stevens, principal of Robinson O'Neal Memorial Primary School, I've been blessed to hear the stories you'll be reading in these pages.

People opened their doors, homes and hearts to me. They also dearly touched my soul.

The people of Virgin Gorda provided the main themes of the book:

*What brought them to the island and what inspired their pursuits?

*What changes have they seen in Virgin Gorda since Laurance Rockefeller created Little Dix Bay, the fabulous resort that launched Virgin Gorda into the 20th century?

*What cultural values have been gained or lost in the transition?

*What progress has been made and at what cost?

In the late 1950s, ecotourism pioneer Laurance Rockefeller, affectionately called the 'quiet Rockefeller,' founded Little Dix Bay and Caneel Bay, her sister resort on St. John in the U.S. Virgin Islands. Since 1993, both resorts have been managed by Rosewood Hotels and Resorts.

Old timers like Waldo O'Neal, ninety, and Elmer George, ninety-two, helped build Little Dix, which first broke ground in 1959. Back then, they said the island was quite primitive. In fact, no roads existed between Virgin Gorda's two towns, The Valley and North Sound, located at opposite sides of the tiny eight-mile island. People traveled by foot, sailboat or donkey. Jobs were almost non-existent. Residents sailed to St. Thomas and other islands to work and sell agricultural products, fish and livestock. Education and health needs were rudimentary at best. In January 1964, Little Dix opened its doors to visitors from all over the world.

That was more than 40 years ago. Imagine the island's transformation from that simple world to what you see today on Virgin Gorda! The island now enjoys full employment. Education has improved with the Bregado Flax Educational Center (with primary and secondary schools) in The Valley and the H. Lavity Stoutt Community College in Tortola. The Nurse Iris O'Neal Clinic is now a full-time medical facility.

Houses once built of wood are now made of stone and cement to better weather the storms. And the island is now filled with major resorts, including Little Dix Bay, the Bitter End Yacht Club, Biras Creek, Saba Rock, Leverick Bay and the Olde Yard Village, not to mention a number of smaller hotels and hundreds of private villas rented out to visitors.

In addition to the influx of tourists, television, the Internet and cruise ships have brought the outside world to this tiny island. Life has changed seemingly overnight. You will hear stories from inhabitants who are both thrilled and concerned about these changes.

Why did I decide to tackle such a wonderful and challenging project? I'm a 15-year 'Non-Belonger' of Virgin Gorda, namely someone who owns a villa and some land on the island. My husband and I were married on this island. My passion for culture led me to be trained to be both a cross-cultural psychotherapist and a professor focused on inter-cultural issues. Therefore, I have been fascinated by both Virgin Gorda's people and their culture. With 15 years' worth of pictures of Virgin Gorda, I've waited for years to put everything I know and love about this island into a book.

With the help of others, namely Julia Leonard (the daughter of the late Sam Leonard, who built our villa), who refers to my husband Mario and me as her "other parents," and Dr. Esmeralda O'Neal, pro-

fessor of linguistics at the H. Lavity Stoutt Community College of Tortola, I have been blessed with the opportunity to meet the people of Virgin Gorda. Some were delighted to speak with me, while others would probably not have shared their stories with me if Julia or Esmeralda had not spoken to them about the importance of this book.

It is my profound hope everyone who participated in this book will find I have faithfully recorded their words and thoughts and will be pleased with and proud of the end product. And to you, my readers, I hope that, in the words of Esther Wheatley, I will "touch your souls" as you read these pages and experience the beauty of Virgin Gorda and its people.

Sincerely,
Joan Massel Soncini, Ph.D.

Virgin Gorda Historical Chronology

Circa 300 A.D.	Archaeologists believe that South American Indians, the Arawaks, Virgin Gorda's first inhabitants, arrive at North Sound.
1493	Christopher Columbus discovers Virgin Gorda and names her the "Fat Virgin."
From 12th-16th Centuries	Carib and Ciboney Indians arrive in Virgin Gorda.
After Columbus	The British come to Virgin Gorda to mine copper ore. Later, British planters arrive with slaves and cattle. Spaniards drive out the British, and introduce tobacco and cotton.
Late 17th Century	First government is established in Spanish Town, then called Penniston.
1735	British gain sovereignty over Virgin Islands. Tortola becomes the center of government. Education provided by Methodist and Anglican missionaries.
1773	First Legislative Council established in Tortola.
1807	Passage of the Slave Trade Act, stipulating plantation owners could no longer obtain slaves from Africa.
1834	Slaves are freed, and now called apprentices.
1838	End of the apprentice system. Once an island of 8,000 people, the end of slavery caused a mass exodus from Virgin Gorda because the island was no longer economically feasible for the middle class.
1840s	Situation in Virgin Gorda: • Little private capital or government spending. • Land appropriated by squatters. • Only primary schooling available.
1947	Tortola opens its first secondary school.

1947	Federation of the Windward (Grenada, St. Lucia, St. Vincent and Dominica) and Leeward Islands (Antigua, St. Kitts, Nevis, Anguilla, Montserrat and the British Virgin Islands).
1956	The British Virgin Islands become a British colony. Since then, there's been debate over whether to remain a colony or pursue self-governance or independence.
1959	Laurance Rockefeller's development of Little Dix Bay begins.
1964	Little Dix Bay opens its doors to visitors all around the world.
1982	Bregado Flax Educational Center opens, offering secondary schooling in Virgin Gorda.
1990	The H. Lavity Stoutt Community College of Tortola opened.
1970s	Nurse Iris O'Neal Clinic opens in Virgin Gorda.

Bibliography:

Dookhan, Isaac. *A History of the British Virgin Islands 1672-1970*. Caribbean Universities Press, Essex, 1975

Lewisohn, Florence. *Tales of Tortola and the British Virgin Islands*. Alroy Printing Co., 1966

Packer, J.E. *British Virgin Islands Articles*. Published May 1971-Feb. 1972.

Penn, Davies Pickering. *Virgin Gorda*. Penn Publishers, East End, Tortola, The Virgin Islands, 1990.

opposite above: Leverick Bay in the foreground and North Sound in the background; right: Taddy Bay Airport with part of The Valley.

XVIII   Virgin Gorda

Chapter One:
Education, Politics, Religion and Health

above: "Free at Last", a quote from Martin Luther King.
Mural painted by Bob George,
located adjacent to the Bregado Flax Educational Centre;

opposite: Top of the Baths and Spring Bay National Park.

above top: Assembly at the Bregado Flax Secondary School;
above bottom: Bregado Flax Educational Centre;

opposite (top and bottom left): Students from the Bregado Flax Primary School,
top and bottom right: Students from the Robinson O'Neal Memorial Primary School.

above top: Miss Lily of St. Mary's Church School;
above bottom: St. Mary's Classroom.

Father Gibson:
Canon Emeritus, the Anglican Church

Coming to the British Virgin Islands:

On August 1, 1956, I sailed into Road Harbor from St. Kitts where I had been working for nearly five years. As my father was born in Guyana in 1883, that gave me a small connection with the West Indies, although I was born in England. I volunteered to go to Guyana after four years in a mining village in England but went to St. Kitts instead.

In 1956 the Bishop visited me in St. Kitts and asked me to move to the Parish of the Virgin Islands, so I became director of St. George's Tortola, which meant I was director of all the Virgin Islands. I came to Virgin Gorda once a month traveling with the doctor during his monthly visits. I'd arrive on a Thursday and stay over until Sunday taking whatever boat returned to Tortola — a nice, big sailing boat, a motorboat, or just a dinghy. One time I returned to Tortola and left at 3 a.m. with two big ladies as passengers. The motor broke down and the poor captain had to row us back to Road Town with just one oar. We did-

Alma Gibson in her Artist Studio

n't reach the East End until 7 a.m. That was the kind of adventure we would have trying to get to Virgin Gorda in those days.

My First Visit to Virgin Gorda:

I arrived at the dock, the old one behind the post office. A small boy who must have been about ten or eleven was there to meet me. He put my bag on his head and marched me up to the school which was located at St. Mary's Church. The catechist (who was also Headmaster of the school) was away so I held services the following Sunday morning. Only one person, a visitor, actually turned up to meet the new rector of the church.

Changes on Virgin Gorda:

When I arrived in 1956 there were only 363 people living in The Valley. That's until Little Dix started. I used to visit every church member on foot when I came over every month.

Almost everything has changed since the early years. It's rather shocking to think how quiet and good everything was and it really isn't the same now because of the growth in population and housing and all the wrong things that can happen in society. It was also very peaceful. It still is, of course.

Meeting Alma, His Wife:

I met Alma when I started work at St. George's. She was 18, far younger than I. She once talked to me about an uncle she was very worried about. She did it so gently and sweetly that I said to myself, "If my period of celibacy was really over, I think Alma would be a wonderful wife."

I was determined not to marry an English woman. I had seen so many priests with English wives, and the priests wanted to stay and work while their wives want-

ed to go back to England. I told myself: "That's not going to happen to me! I'm getting a West Indian wife so I can stay here." We were married on Feb. 4, 1959. It was a great deal of trouble, of course – a white priest, a black Virgin Island girl. Many said it wouldn't work at all, as we were completely unsuited to each other.

First we adopted Angela. Then our son was born but he was ill, and sadly died when he was six. The Lord replaced him exactly ten years later with our daughter, Joy. We've never had any problems whatsoever on racial grounds. Our 50th anniversary is coming up. It's been a perfect marriage.

Becoming a Member of the British Empire:

You ask about my becoming a MBE or "Member of the Most Excellent Order of the British Empire" and a canon of the Anglican Church. Just before my retirement in 1992, and to my astonishment, the deputy governor in Tortola told me the Queen wanted to make me a MBE. My immediate response was, "Me? What have I done to done to get a MBE?" He said, "Well, you taught at school and you've done a lot in the community. Will you accept it?" Of course, I said!

Alma and I went to Buckingham Palace in England where I received this honor. Then the bishop told me he'd like to make me a canon of the cathedral. He said he was quite glad I accepted for he feared I would be rather humble and turn it down.

I celebrated my 50th anniversary of work in the Virgin Islands this past month, and my 60th ordination anniversary is coming up. Then, of course, Alma and I will celebrate 50 wonderful years together in 2009.

Gracia Stevens: Principal of the Robinson O'Neal Memorial Primary School at North Sound

Early Years:

I was born on this island in my grandma's house, which is still standing on North Sound. I got my primary education here, starting school at six – not sooner – since I was tiny and the roads were really bad to travel on. On my fifteenth birthday I didn't leave school like the others did. I was well-behaved and the head teacher, a gentleman by the name of Obed Malone, wanted me to be a teacher, as he felt I had what it took. It wasn't my first choice. I really wanted to be a chef, maybe at the newly opened Little Dix Bay. However, my grandmother insisted I take the teaching position. I went into it at sixteen and I'm still there at sixty!

I taught kindergarten for thirteen years and then I went to Antigua for a year, where I received my teacher training certificate in 1974.

I came back to the new school building at North Sound first as a teacher, then acting principal, followed by becoming the head

teacher in 1980 and since then I've been the principal of the school.

I didn't want to teach but I came to love it very much.

Life in North Sound:

There have been some enormous changes in North Sound starting with the roads. They used to be just track roads – stony paths – and it was difficult to get from one end of the island to the other. As a little girl, I remember on a Friday afternoon after school, I'd walk to The Valley and buy certain things and walk back on Saturday. That walk took maybe an hour. Often we'd ride a donkey which was the only means of carrying loads on the island at the time besides carrying them on your head!

The main changes on the island occurred after Little Dix opened. Since we had quite a number of visitors from off-shore there had to be some development to accommodate them. The roads were built around 1967 opening The Valley to vehicular traffic. Then electricity was a problem. We had to burn little lamps with oil. Walking in the dark was extremely dangerous because you were walking on stony paths and you could fall.

Before the opening of Little Dix people from North Sound usually found employment in St. Thomas. The young boys left school when they were fifteen or sixteen. They were employed on small sailing sloops with older men as the captains. They took boats to St. Thomas loaded with charcoal – one of the island's main industries. There was a spot at Gun Creek pretty close to the dock where people used to pile up the bags of coal and keep a check of who had ten or twenty bags. These bags were loaded onto the boats and sold in St. Thomas. Other products including eggs, fish and cattle were sold at St. Thomas, St. Croix and as far away as St. Barts. Off they would go in these little sloops. It was amazing how they made it: driven by the wind without engines. Young women

often went to St. Thomas to work with people who hired them to wash, iron, cook and clean. I was fortunate to get a job right in the community here in North Sound.

Technology, Transportation and Communication:

There have been changes in our lives since then. I feel the influence of television (if not used properly) prevents children from studying or learning. They stay up too late at night and then can't function at school. Computers can also be harmful when children spend too much time with the wrong things. Yet computers open our children's minds. We have a lab with about 19 state-of-the-art computers. They were donated to us by Mr. Bert Houwer, the owner of Biras Creek.

Another major change is transportation. We have buses, cars and boats. Now you can get to Tortola in twenty-five minutes and even right on the hour sometimes!

There was a time when there were no telephones and the only means of communicating was by letter – which could take weeks to get. E-mailing has made contact with people far away possible. I have a daughter right now in Germany. She's in the military and I can see her sitting in her living room. I can talk with her.

I have three daughters and one son. My son works at the front office of Little Dix. One daughter is a teacher and the other works in information technology systems. All of them have benefited from a good education, which makes me very proud of them.

above top: Ms. Darleen Henry of the Robinson O'Neal Memorial Primary School;
above bottom: Ms. Norma Creque of the Robinson O'Neal Memorial Primary School.

Louis Walters: Former Minister of Education for the British Virgin Islands

Becoming a Teacher:

When I was growing up in Virgin Gorda, there wasn't an opportunity to go to high school so I had to get a job. I could be a pharmacist or a teacher. My parents said, "Be a teacher!" I had just finished my primary education in The Valley, sixth grade, and this was way back in 1948 when I was 14. So I became a teacher in Virgin Gorda. I worked without pay, by the way, until 1951 when I started at $9.62 a month in U.S. dollars.

I was trained by school principals. We had to work in classes all day long and these classes were a challenge. Our schools were really a one-room classroom, with all ages together. You're sitting here, they're sitting there and everybody's screaming at the top of their voices to get attention.

Learning was by memorization. Basically it was the three "Rs" (reading, riting, and rithmatic). Looking back today I don't think we understood much of what we were doing.

For example, I went to the United Kingdom

above: Lynn Weekes' Class of the Bregado Flax Educational Centre.

and sailed across the English Channel to France. Well, I had learned about the White Cliffs of Dover but had no idea they were real cliffs. I stood there, watched them and I said to myself, "Oh my goodness, how marvelous!"

During my time as a teacher we simply sat in front of the classroom with a paper, a book, a blackboard and chalk. It's not something I'm very proud of doing, because I feel I didn't do justice to the people I taught, leaving them with a void in their lives that had to be filled. Unfortunately, there is little change in many of our schools, which I find very sad.

Moving Away From the British Virgin Islands:

It's difficult for our students to find jobs after they are educated abroad. They often want to be a head of a department or something of that nature. Some are old enough to say they have ideas and knowledge of technology and what's going on in the world. They think they should get important positions and they get frustrated because they can't get a promotion quickly enough. So we have problems. They're not really running away from the country, but opportunities for

development and upward mobility are few and far between. So they go and some never come back. We are suffering a brain drain in the Virgin Islands. We train a lot of people and they leave. For this reason, I think a great percentage of our teachers are expatriates from Guyana, Trinidad and other islands.

Early Life in Virgin Gorda:

Life was tough in Virgin Gorda. You lived on what you were able to produce from the land. People fished and farmed. A few of them had cattle, goats, pigs and chickens around the house. They baked their own goods and they made their own foods without having to exchange a simple dime, since everything was done by barter. We only started using American money after the war and the building of the Panama Canal. At that point trade started with the U.S. Virgin Islands- particularly in St. Thomas.

I'll tell you the story of my very first pen. My mother gave me a hen that laid ten eggs, which I then sold in St. Thomas for fifty U.S. cents. In those days, we had the Sears Roebuck catalog. Since I was in the teaching business I ordered my first fountain pen after I sold the eggs. I didn't have enough to buy the pen – which cost sixty-seven cents – so I had to beg for extra money to buy my pen. It was a hard life.

Politics and Becoming Minister of Education:

I ended up in politics, which really was not intentional. I became minister of education for the British Virgin Islands for eight years, from 1986-94.

I'll explain how that happened. I took a higher post in the West End as my first assignment outside of Virgin Gorda. I ended up becoming acting head principal at Anegada, where I remained for only about seven or eight months because it was so isolated in those days. Then I went to college in Antigua and went wherever there was a vacancy.

I got married in East End. After the wedding, I said to myself, "No, no, no, I can't take this moving around anymore." I needed to settle down somewhere, so I tendered my resignation just before Little Dix Bay opened in 1964. I had just finished a correspondence course in accounting from the United Kingdom and requested an accounting position at Little Dix. The manager said all he could offer at that time was a posi-

tion as captain of the dining room staff. I did that for three years when Little Dix closed down for the summer.

I was then offered the job of headmaster for the St. Mary's School in Virgin Gorda. After a couple of years I moved on to a private school in Road Town, Tortola. I said, "Look, if I am going to teach here I have to get experience and more modern training outside this country." So after a year I was allowed to go to the University of Birmingham in England. When I returned I became an administrator and two years later I was transferred up the ladder to higher positions.

In the mid-1980 I started my business in Virgin Gorda which consists presently of some buildings. Chez Bamboo is in one of them. That's mine. I resigned from administration, lived in East End but visited Virgin Gorda from time to time.

During this time a group of people got together and asked me if I'd like to go into politics. I said the only way I'd be interested would be if they would guarantee their support. I entered politics just like that and stayed in it for eight years as minister of education. That is my story. Since then I've just relaxed and worked on my garden, which I love.

below left: Principal George, Pastor Silvia Rhymer, parents and students of the Robinson O'Neal Memorial Primary School; right: Esmeralda O'Neal and family.

The Honorable Ralph T. O'Neal: Education, Teaching and Politics

Ralph and wife, Edris O'Neal, Anglican minister

My Educational Background:

I was fortunate to get a scholarship to St. Kitts. However, my father was ill and my mother couldn't raise the money to send me. My father died in July 1947 and in August I was offered a job as a teacher in Tortola. I could earn $8 a month and stay with a friend of my mother. But this cost $10 a month. My mother found the extra $2, which she used to help further my education.

Later in 1948 I applied for and received a British gov-

ernment scholarship to be educated in St. Kitts. You had to agree to be a teacher when you were done. After three years I came back and taught from 1951 to 1956.

Later I became principal at the North Sound Robinson O'Neal Memorial Primary School. At that time it was the most backward school in the territory. They never had a child pass the primary school exam. The first year I was there two passed! Teaching up there was a pleasure, as parents and friends (whether or not they had children) were so involved.

From Teaching to Politics:

While I was in North Sound I had a lot of free time to read. I read about how the people of Bermuda were getting on. This made me look at our own situation here in the BVIs. The history book stated cattle and agriculture were the mainstay of our economy, but I found that wasn't so. The mainstay of the economy was funds people brought back home from jobs abroad in Cuba, Puerto Rico, the Dominican Republic, St. Thomas and the United States.

I thought about how we suffered from long droughts and said to myself, "No! We've got to find something better to help our people, our country!" I had long conversations about these issues with my friend, Mr. George Cecil Rhymer. We'd talk about Virgin Gorda's future and he would say, "Well, look at that nice harbor you have up there. It's going to be developed, Teacher!"

When I finished with teaching I came to the conclusion it would be a good thing for me to go into politics. But first I had to work in the civil service and learn the intricacies of government if I really wanted to change things.

I believe I was able to contribute something toward that end! I got a lot of joy and satisfaction from it. For instance, I watched as people got scholarships toward furthering their studies – some becoming lawyers, doctors and engineers. And you know, there's even one from North Sound now, Janice Charles Creque, who is a judge in Anguilla.

below: Bregado Flax Primary School opens with a daily prayer.

Martha Holder:
Co-founder of the Valley Day Primary School

Our first visit to Virgin Gorda was in 1971. We fell in love with everything about it, especially the people. Each year we came back and stayed at the Olde Yard Inn. We needed to get away from the intense pressure of our very busy lives. For seventeen years we'd owned and directed a year-round children's center in Denver with multiple programs to meet the educational and recreational needs of about 100 children (ages three to twelve). Running the school was hard but very rewarding work.

In 1997 we decided to buy land and build a home in Virgin Gorda and soon found the

Martha Holder with her much loved husband, Gene, who so sadly passed away.

perfect spot in a little neighborhood on Handsome Bay. We wanted to be part of real island life and the community.

Then things just started falling into place. Just as our house in Virgin Gorda was nearing completion a staff member asked us to sell her our school. At the same time we received calls from people in Virgin Gorda encouraging us to open a private primary school. Then the manager of Little Dix Bay Hotel called to say the hotel owner would provide a little building near the jetty for a school. We said "Yes" and started packing.

In the fall of 1979 the Valley Day School opened with five small children. As our numbers grew we needed another teacher. We asked island resident Barbara Craig to join us. She volunteered for 11 years as part of our wonderful teaching team. We couldn't have done it without her. The school had a wonderful mix of children – multiracial, multicultural and multi-linguistic. The children learned not only their lessons but also how to get along with one another. The greatest lesson they learned was that we were much more alike than different. Over time our small student body became a family.

When Valley Day School was about a year old parents of public school students started asking us to help their children too. Gene and I then started an after-school tutoring program three days a week. Before long the children were asking for help. Some came for a few weeks and some a few years. Gene also set up a G.E.D. (for a secondary school degree) class before the high school was built on Virgin Gorda. Gene and I always considered ourselves educators. Our philosophy stressed the importance of learning and feeling good about themselves.

In 1996 we passed the school on to Jan Morash, who continues today as its headmistress. For over 17 years we worked with many wonderful children who have done well. It has been such a joy to watch them grow up into adulthood and contribute to this beautiful island we love so much. When Gene passed away last year so many people came to share their love and their hugs with me. We've received much more than we've given. It's been a magical life!

below left: The late Gene Holder;
right: Valley Day Primary School students.

Ingrid Waters: Guidance Counselor at the Bregado Flax Primary School

I was born and raised here as a single child from a single-parent home. I grew up with my mom, Grace Waters, who is Director of Reservations and Guest Relations at Little Dix Bay. She has been my inspiration over the years. I got into guidance counseling because I loved the kids and wanted to help them develop into something positive and inspiring for our community. Over the years we have adopted, perhaps, too much of an American lifestyle. I think we need to go back to being more people-oriented. Yet, the community is a warm and caring society and I simply love being here on this little island.

Bringing Back Our Culture:

We have media and television and this creates difficulties. But many of us are trying to bring back our culture especially in the schools. We're trying to bring back the history of where we came from and encourage young people to sit and take their time, obey rules and regulations and make society a lot safer and happier.

I always encourage people to get to know this side of the world because I think it's one of nature's hidden secrets. Come on down, appreciate what we have to offer and get to know our culture!

above left: Nurse Iris O'Neal Clinic, The Valley;

left: Valley Methodist Church, The Valley;

above: Church of God Holiness, North Sound.

Chapter Two:
The Baths and Boulders

above: Devil's Bay;
above right: The Baths.

The Baths and Boulders

According to the book, "The Story of the Boulders," by Charles A. Ratte, the famous Baths of Virgin Gorda's southwestern shore are made up of enormous boulders resulting from geologic processes. Sometimes several stories high, many of these boulders have special names such as 'rounded boulder,' 'pitted or fluted boulder' and 'hollow boulder.'

One of the most exciting things to do while visiting The Baths is to walk through the boulders – beginning at The Baths' beach area. Stooping very low through

left: A glorious, natural Bath;
middle two: Neptune's Hideaway;
right: The Baths ladder.

Chapter 2

a rock formation, one walks toward the most famous "Bath", a glorious, natural Bath with boulders one to two stories high. Then on toward the highest boulder, "Neptune's Hideway", climbing up and down the various ladders and coming out at the gorgeous Devil's Bay.

After exploring The Baths and Devil's Bay, my husband and I often go to The Top of the Baths to visit our friends Charlene and Norman Henderson where we eat at their restaurant and shop at the stores.

The Baths and Boulders

above: Top of the Baths' mural,
painted by Joseph Hodge;
left: Top of the Baths at night;
opposite: The ladies who lunch with
Charlene Henderson.

Chapter 2

Charlene Henderson:
Owner of The Top of the Baths Restaurant and The Oil Nut Bay Development in North Sound

Charlene's Parents and The Baths:

There were few economic opportunities for people here. My grandparents were both from Virgin Gorda and they moved to the Dominican Republic in the 1800s. My father was Dr. Eric I. O'Neal, a surgeon and pioneer in health care in the U.S. Virgin Islands. My Mom was Clara O'Neal a business woman. My dad was born on Virgin Gorda, but his family returned to the Dominican Republic when he was a baby and remained there until he was 9 or 10. His family then moved to St. Thomas. However, my grandparents instilled in my father a genuine love and appreciation for Virgin Gorda.

My father practiced medicine in New York until 1948, when my parents returned to St. Thomas to set up his private practice. He took great pride in bringing friends every month or two to Virgin Gorda to experience the islands and its people, and of course to see The Baths, which is a monument known all over the world.

In those days, traveling from St. Thomas to Virgin Gorda was planned a month ahead of time. You had to bring provisions because there weren't any grocery stores. When I came here with my father, there wasn't even electricity. There were perhaps 100 people in The Valley, with the only other community, North Sound, on the other side of the island, with no road in between.

Devil's Bay, The Baths, and Spring Bay were always owned by local families, and my father purchased The Baths from his cousins in 1952.

The Baths were always a place for social occasions here in Virgin Gorda. Eventually in 1987, the BVI government acquired the beach area and The Baths from my family. My father had a dream, well, a plan. He wanted this gem to be passed on to the people of his native land and always open for others to come and visit and experience the wonder of the property.

My father had many opportunities to sell the property. People would contact him and say, "Name your price." He'd say, "No, no, no. If it doesn't belong to our family, then it will go to the people of the British Virgin Islands, and in particular, the people of Virgin Gorda." The dollar wasn't important to him, which I respect a lot.

Her Family's Return to Virgin Gorda:

In the early 1960s, my family decided to return to Virgin Gorda and build a restaurant with shops. However, negotiations with the government over The Baths took about 20 years, so we weren't allowed to build on any part of the property. The final settlement took place in 1990, and we were finally able to go ahead with our plans to build with our friend, Sam Leonard. Sam was just so instrumental in helping us decide where to build and how best to represent Virgin Gorda. At first, we were going to lease everything out. But Sam said we really should come and live on Virgin Gorda. Norman gave up teaching Biology in the evenings at the University of The Virgin Islands and his day-time position as a Biology instructor at the Charlotte Amalie High School. As for me, I eventually gave up my position as a Social Worker for the Family Resource Center for victims of abuse and crime.

We're blessed to be here. It's a privilege to live on Virgin Gorda. My mom was fortunate to live long enough to see it. Unfortunately my dad passed away, but I feel like he's looking down and guiding us every step of the way.

My children have helped us. Erica works in the real estate office. Eric's kids are in St. Thomas. Omar, my grandson, says, "Grandma, Virgin Gorda is a magical place."

When they come, there's no time for TV, no time for those little handheld games. It's all about going outside and exploring, so they spend their whole time outside. So we're glad, and really happy to have them here.

Changes in Virgin Gorda:

I remember coming here as a child and visiting my grandmother. We would spend at least a month during the summer on Virgin Gorda.

At that time, there were a lot of cashew nut trees and whelks growing in The Baths. You didn't have as many people visiting so there was more privacy. But this is the price you pay for progress. Of course you have more economic opportunities for people living here, and that unfortunately brings overcrowding on some days at The Baths. But what is good about it is people don't have to leave the island, go live someplace else, and contribute to someone else's development. They can stay here and bring their children up in a safe and loving environment because Virgin Gorda is a very special place. My grandchildren now share the same love I have for Virgin Gorda, the same love that my father had for it, as well as his mother and father, and that's a pretty special thing.

above: The Baths' beach area;
right: Albert Wheatley and sons at the
Top of the Baths.

The Baths and Boulders

Chapter Three:
The Valley and Spanish Town

above: Flags at Spanish Town;
above right: By Buck's.

Waldo O'Neal:
Worked on Original Construction of Little Dix Bay

How long have I been here? Since Jan. 13, 1916, the day I was born! We had 10 children in our family. Ralph is my younger brother, and I'm uncle to Caryl (principal of the Bregado Flax Secondary School), Icilma, and Esmeralda O'Neal. Charlene O'Neal Henderson is my cousin.

Like many others, I only had a primary school education, since there was no secondary school in Virgin Gorda at that time. My dad was a carpenter, but he also had a lot of livestock. We all had to help him.

Jobs? There were no jobs here at all, so I went sailing. During World War II, I went to St. Thomas to help build the Bournefield Military Base, and there I learned how to be a skilled carpenter.

Oh, and from 1957-60, when I was 41-44 years old, I joined a political party and was elected to the Legislative Council.

We didn't know about Laurance Rockefeller until he built Little Dix. The Jackson Hole Preserve Agency purchased land from folks for Little Dix, which opened in 1964.

What was life like before Little Dix? Things were so slow in Virgin Gorda. Everyone had to go away to Santo Domingo, St. Kitts, St Martin and Antigua to make a living. Charcoal, fishing and cattle were the only ways to make money.

Rockefeller was greeted with open arms by all in the British Virgin Islands. Why? Jobs! – although they mostly brought in people from Europe and other islands, and only a few of the locals could work to their standards.

We earned $16.80 per week in St. Thomas during World War II. Rockefeller paid us $60 a week. What a difference! I was lucky, since I learned how to do good work in St Thomas. So I helped build the hotel, with what we called the English "finishers," who were really trained.

How did the island change after Little Dix? Crazy, full speed! In the beginning we had four pickup trucks on the island. I walked back and forth in the morning, had lunch at home, and then returned in the afternoon.

Now, there are cars everywhere.

Progress has good and bad sides. On the plus side, look at my house. It used to be about 20 by 14 feet, and I just built it up bigger and better. I think the best part is education is much better today, and I'm really pleased about that. Now we have Bregado Flax Secondary School in Virgin Gorda and a college in Tortola. We're lucky now because people can find good jobs.

Author's Note:

At the end of our interview, my very first interview for this book, I asked Waldo: "Was there conflict between wealthy newcomers, like the folks who came to Little Dix and those who built villas on Virgin Gorda, and the locals?"

He responded, "Fortunately it didn't happen like that. We're better off because of labor and money."

In conclusion, Waldo said, "I put in a $20 bill at church, and this guy asked me why I didn't put in more. I remember when I only could put in one cent!"

below: Welcoming folks at Taddy Bay Airport.

Virgin Gorda: The Way we Were, 1960

above left: Looking towards Gorda Peak from
Handsome Bay;
left: Looking towards the present Yacht Harbour,
with the Recreation Ground in the foreground;
above: Looking towards the Valley, with Handsome
Bay in the left of the foreground.
All photos by Euan McFarland, circa 1960.

above top: Government Dock;
above left: Bath & Turtle restaurant; above right: Kaunda's Kysy Tropix.

Chapter 3

Elmer and Viva George:
Sailor, Carpenter at Little Dix and his Wife, the Oldest Resident of Virgin Gorda

Author's Note:

I heard Viva George was the oldest resident of Virgin Gorda, and her husband, Elmer, spent the earliest years on Virgin Gorda and helped build Little Dix Bay. So I wanted to interview Viva, 101, and her 92-year-old husband Elmer to hear their story.

Elmer answered the phone, and invited me over for a visit. My husband, Mario, joined me. We arrived at the top of a hill, were about to turn left, then around a corner and look for an open gate. These were the only directions we had, so of course we got lost. Luckily, there's always someone around who can help you reach your destination.

We find their house. The garden is impeccable. Elmer is working away at a hedge. "See, I'm working!" he says, before inviting us in. Unfortunately, Viva isn't in great shape. She recently fell and was unable to join us.

Elmer tells me about his life. He was born in Virgin

Gorda and went to St. Thomas with his friend Waldo O'Neal during the war in the 1940s. Then, he worked in Manhattan at the Hospital for Joint Diseases until the 1980s. He met Viva when he was 70 at the Methodist Church in New York where they both sang in the choir. Viva, who was 79 at the time and a widow, was also born in Virgin Gorda. Elmer returned to Virgin Gorda for four years and then brought his Viva back to the island after they got married.

Elmer and Viva's story is, indeed, a special love story. They are devoted to one another, and Elmer is very proud of his wife. After all, she's 101 years old!

This articulate, warm gentleman spoke about the changes that have taken place in Virgin Gorda. He shared an insider/outsider view of the island. Since he lived in New York for so many years before returning to Virgin Gorda, Elmer agreed with his friend Waldo that there wasn't much on the island before Laurance Rockefeller came in 1959. There were no roads, no cars, no jobs and no schools. He only had positive things to say about the island and said that improvements in housing, transportation, education and healthcare came after the establishment of Little Dix Bay.

I asked if I could take his picture at the end of the interview. "Oh no, I'm dressed for gardening," Elmer said.

"Could you please come back when I am appropriately dressed for a picture?"

So Sunday – Church day – was the day. When I called that morning to set up a time to take his picture, I spoke to Viva. She moved me greatly with her comment, "I have a lot of problems, but I thank the good Lord for every day he gives me."

I went to the Methodist Valley Church (where, coincidently, my husband and I were married) and gave Elmer a ride home. He was dressed in a three-piece suit and hat. Although it was too hot to walk comfortably, he often made that trip on foot when he couldn't get a ride.

At home, Viva was eating breakfast with her caretaker. She was a bit shocked by my presence, so I sat down on the couch. When Elmer came over, I asked him if Viva would join him for the picture. He talked to her – I hoped he wasn't pressuring her – and then I heard her say, "You let a stranger in our house. Why did you do that? Pictures? I don't want any pictures."

Elmer was gentle and eventually convinced her. They posed for me. After telling Viva and Elmer stories about my many connections to the people on Virgin Gorda, especially Reverend Franklin Roberts, Viva invited me to return any time. I no longer felt like a stranger.

Chapter 3

Tina Goschler: Owner of Guavaberry Homes

My family must be one of the first expatriate, white families in the British Virgin Islands. My grandfather came to Tortola in 1920 with his sons. My father left for Scotland to be educated and then worked for the Air Force before returning home in 1957 with his wife and three kids. In 1965, my parents decided to sell their hotel – Treasure Isle – on Tortola and start Guavaberry Homes on Virgin Gorda, on property that my grandparents purchased in 1937 as a 25th wedding anniversary present to each other.

Little Dix opened its doors in 1964, so my parents first worked there while building Guavaberry Homes. By 1969, they had five houses to manage and rent to visitors. Eventually they worked full-time at Guavaberry, and added new homes.

I have fond memories of what I call the "good old days," when I was a kid. It was tough, but better. I remember the roads were not paved and when it rained they would wash out. I'd walk in front of my Dad's car (he had the second on the island) to see how far I'd go down in the mud. I don't know which was more valuable – me or his car!

First, we lived in a temporary three-bedroom trailer, but then it became permanent. We had no electricity, but we had this generator, which Dad turned on early morning and then closed late night. No TV!

Race? We didn't face many real issues. We were one of the few white families on Tortola and Virgin Gorda, where the local people were unused to seeing a white face.

When we wanted to go over to Tortola, we'd take the Chocolate Queen, which at that time took two hours. The ladies would sit below, but I'd get seasick, so I'd sit with my father when he was there.

After attending school in Puerto Rico, I returned to Virgin Gorda in 1979 and ran Guavaberry with my parents, although they were certainly in charge. In January, I met Ludwig Goschler at The Bath & Turtle. He was German-born and came over to work with the North South Yacht Charters. We married in November, 1979.

In 1984, my husband and I took over the management of Guavaberry Homes. My father died in 1985, and my mother let me run it. We've improved a lot with new houses, 19 so far, and we manage private villas, too. We added an office and lounge two years ago.

We have two daughters who have benefited from living on this wonderful, safe island. The only drawback has been we knew at a certain age, after their studies at The Valley Day School, that we would send them away to Canada for schooling.

Changes over time? Well, the island has grown so quickly, and not all for the better. I wish we had stayed the same. TV and folks from off-island have brought their values and cultures to our island. As I see it, that has caused a loss of culture, which was very good here, especially respect for others, and above all, for the elders.

below left: Wild bougainvillea;
right: Julia Leonard.

Sam Leonard and Chris Yates,
Builders and Owners of Leverick Bay

Author's Note:

Sam Leonard had a central role in the development of Virgin Gorda. Born on April 19, 1949, Sam died tragically in a freak accident on Jan. 12, 1995.

Chris Yates, his partner at Leonard and Yates Construction Company, came to the British Virgin Islands in 1968 as an electrical engineer from England.

Here, she remembers him fondly.

Chris Yates:

In late 1976 I had a project to build seven round houses at Leverick Bay and needed a sub-contractor to build the cisterns. That's how I met Sam. Of the three people I talked to about the project, Sam was the only one who said he could do the project on time and budget instead of giving 50 reasons why it could not be done. Sam completed the project on time and we formed Leonard and Yates Construction Company to work on

above top: Chris and her dogs;
above bottom: Sam at Leverick Bay.

Chapter 3

future projects as equal partners. From that time on, we were business partners in everything we did until his tragic death in 1995.

Sam always said the key to our success was that we were best friends as well as business partners. He made up in common sense what I lacked, and I made up in book learning what he lacked. We had a unique system of solving our differences. When we disagreed on a subject, we would write 10 to 20-page letters to each other stating our positions until we reached a compromise – but usually we did what we wanted to do anyway!

As the construction company grew, Sam diversified into other areas. He was already an accomplished musician and frequently entertained company clients and friends at parties. We started a property development company and developed Leverick Bay Hotel and Marina. He was the driving force behind the Virgin Gorda Quarry, where he died in an accident. We developed the Mahoe Bay Estates, which is now one of the most successful villa developments in the British Virgin Islands. Sam was a person who was loved and respected by all members of the community and never said a bad word about anyone.

Author's Note:

Sam Leonard was loved by just about everyone who knew him. But he was especially loved by those who survived him: his four children, Julia, Sammy, Shellie, and Joy Leonard; Franka Pickering, with whom Sam shared two children and his life; his partner Chris Yates, and too many friends to name.

During Sam's Funeral Service on Jan. 21, 1995, at the Road Town Methodist Church, the Honorable Ralph T. O'Neal delivered a touching and beautiful eulogy for Sam, written by his beloved daughter Julia Leonard:

Sam was a true lover of life, and lived his life to the fullest. His young and tender

years were spent with his family at their home in Sea Cow's Bay. Even before the age of 7, Sam demonstrated to the frustration of his mother the level of his creativity as an individual. When he was 5 years old and first saw airplanes flying, he thought they were men with wings in the sky. So he decided if he would then make some wings like a bird he should be able to do the same thing. He went to the top of the family home, tied his wings to his hands, and feet. Sam then took off, only to land in one of the trees in the yard. He was knocked unconscious.

Sam started out sailing at sea. After a short apprenticeship with Brother Joshua Smith, he left with the late Captain Carlton de Castro for six years at sea. Sam became the cook and the mate to the captain. After sailing on the Tropic Star, Sam began to sail with Captain Elwin Flax, who brought him to Virgin Gorda. While there, he began to work at Little Dix Bay Hotel and Marina.

The word "talented" seems to be inadequate to express the true nature of this man, "a self-made man." His daughter, Julia, often asked him, "How did you learn to do so many different things: heavy equipment work, mechanics, architecture, civil engineering, and playing music – the piano, organ, guitar and bass?" He would often reply, "I have read a little, watched and learned something all in the process of teaching myself."

During Sam's early days of sailing with Captain Carlton, he started his musical career by teaching himself how to play the guitar. Later he learned how to play the keyboard instruments and bass, and started to sing more seriously. He then began to share his inspiration by forming a band

and singing with his Aunt Christiana Thomas in the band known as The Vibrations. With this band, he wrote and arranged a number of songs and music. The most well-known are "Don't Let No Other Man Fool You," and "I Thank God for the Angel, That He Sent Me from Above." This band had many successes, among others, touring throughout the Caribbean with famous singers, such as Sparrow, Milo and the Kings and Arrow.

In 1967 Sam met and fell in love with Mrs. Lydia Lettsome Jackson, and later on in 1970, they had his first-born, Julia. Then in 1974, Sam married his dear wife, the late Mrs. Joan Flax Leonard, second daughter of Captain and Mrs. Elwin Flax. Joan had Sam's first two sons, the eldest of which passed away soon after birth, and the sec-

ond, Ricardo Samuel Leonard, in 1976. Sadly, Sam lost his wife to illness at the young age of 35. His next son, Sheldon, was born on Nov. 15,1980, and on March 21, 1991, Sam and Franka had their daughter, Joy. Sam was a man who simply loved his children around him.

Sam, you will be remembered as someone who knew what you wanted. You lived your life to the fullest as you believed it should be lived. If, or whenever you had a problem, the world would not know, for you always gave out joy, laughter and thus happiness. There were always the kind words, the genuine smile and the thoughtfulness. It simply appeared that once the sun was shining and your stomach full, no matter what, life simply couldn't have been better.

opposite (clockwise from top left):
Earl and his three sons; Kaunda Leonard; Jolene and Gunther with adopted son; Miss Gracie.

Virgin Gorda: The Way we Were, 1960

above top: View of former salt pond, where Virgin Gorda Yacht Harbour now stands, facing towards Tortola;

above left: Road from St. Thomas Bay leading to Handsome Bay;

above right: Road being built leading towards Spanish Town and Little Dix Bay on the right;

opposite page clockwise from top left: 1960's cricket game;

Building the foundations of what is now the Flying Iguana Restaurant; St. Mary's School children.

All photos by Euan McFarland, circa 1960.

Joe Giacinto: Owner of Dive BVI

I was born in Long Island, New York. I'd been visiting my brother Mike, who has been living on Great Camanoe, since 1968. At the time I was an IBM salesman, and my brother wanted me to work with his construction company, but I wasn't interested. Then Mike purchased the lease on Marina Cay with a group of people and planned to run the hotel. So when he asked me to be resident manager of Marina Cay, I said yes, and came in 1972.

Since I was a scuba diver I started a diving program at Marina Cay. I was friendly with Bert Kilbride – who was the old sage of diving in the British Virgin Islands – and I started to fill in for him when he went on vaca-tion. He started Dive BVI and offered it to me with a location in the Yacht Harbour. So I moved here to Virgin Gorda in October 1975. The business is now incorporated – Dive BVI Limited.

The program started as a two-person operation. It was very hard work. But it was a friendly, easy envi-ronment so I met everybody. It was a nice place to be. Business has grown, and there are now three loca-tions – two at Virgin Gorda and one at Pusser's at Marina Cay. We also have an area at Little Dix Bay, too, and we take people out diving from all the hotels on Virgin Gorda.

It was easier to own a business back then, when I first came here 30 years ago. It took me six months to become a resident, but some 29 years to become naturalized as a citizen and a "Belonger." I now have dual citizenship.

Development in Virgin Gorda

I hate to see too much development, but I don't see it as intrusive on Virgin Gorda. I see us as "low silhouette" growth. It's not high rises, it's not densely populated. There are about 4,000 people on the island now, so from that standpoint it's good.

I was invited to be a member of the Tourist Board.

We've been working on developing a cruise-ship policy to help Virgin Gorda with its growth and progress.

My Brother Mike:

I followed my brother Mike in so many ways, beginning with going to Notre Dame. We were both athletic and he convinced me to join the Marine Corps. Later I followed him to the British Virgin Islands. Mike was a builder, an artist, a talented sculptor. He was also involved in women's fashion, and that's how he met Rose – his second wife. He loved life, but he left it early. He was only 52 when he died.

opposite and above:

Original houses on Virgin Gorda.

Chapter Four:
North Sound

left top: Arriving at North Sound; below: The road toward Leverick Bay;
above: The Bars at North Sound and Gun Creek.

Bert Kilbride: Diver, Treasure Hunter and Owner of the Original Saba Rock, North Sound

Gayla Kilbride

Author's Note:

Bert was born on March 8, 1914, in Springfield, Massachusetts. He's been treasure hunting since he was born. He used to dive and retrieve rings, watches and necklaces that tourists had lost at sea.

Bert's Story:

In 1953 I was building schools in Miami. I was general superintendent and my company went down to St. Croix to build the Kingshill Elementary School. I ended up staying there, building houses and developing land. My wife had a boat, so we came to the Virgin Islands in 1958.

After a year or so I bought Mosquito Island. I built Drake's Anchorage as a dive resort – and it was one of the first dive operations in the area. We had a restaurant and my wife would cook for the guests while I was out diving. We bought some boats and rented them out.

I sold the island and bought Saba Rock, transferring my diving business there in

above top: View of North Sound from High Road;

above bottom: Boys kayaking at the Bitter End.

North Sound

above: Scenes at Leverick Bay.

Chapter 4

Gayla Kilbride

1969–1970. At that time, Jean-Michel Cousteau was working on Project Ocean Search, and leading diving expeditions all over the world. He'd take 60 people or so for two weeks of diving every year. So one year, Jean was in St. Thomas and looking for whales. I knew where the whales were, toward Anegada. So I called him up and that's how we met. I showed them the whales, and Cousteau even made a film about me. Later on, he returned with 60 people, and I took care of them for two weeks, giving him the 20 dives which were promised in the contract. He returned after that even though he always said he never went anywhere twice. Why? He said this was the first place that he got every dive that was promised. It went on for 13 years. Cousteau never went anywhere else. He even made a movie of me!

Life on Saba Rock:

It was wonderful. Gayla, my present wife, had a great restaurant on Saba Rock. On Thanksgiving, she'd cook 12 turkeys, inviting boat people over for a free meal.

I got a government contract to find a big boat that was wrecked on the reef. We picked up 138 wreck site readings along the whole reef. I was one of the first divers when the Rhone went down, because there weren't any scuba divers and the natives didn't dive, so they didn't even get in the water. The Navy came down and blasted it until it sank. I got the people who filmed the movie "The Deep" to do the main part of the film on location at the Rhone, and I got my former wife, Jackie, a job as a double for Jacqueline Bisset.

Change on the Island:

Over time, more people came down to dive. I had five boats and my three sons were working with me. We had one of the biggest scuba diving operations in the British Virgin Islands. Cousteau publicized it, and everyone who came sent more people. We showed them a good time. I was able to train beginners to dive in three hours. I called it my "resort course," which started when we were still at Drake's Anchorage. Now, people from all over the world use my resort course for training and certifying people. I even got a nice statue, a reward, for my contribution to diving instruction.

Gayla Kilbride:

Bert was one of the first people I met in the British Virgin Islands in 1982. This guy said, "I'll introduce you to Bert Kilbride," like it was a big deal or something. He was like a celebrity. Thirteen days later I jumped ship – aiming to stay here and find a windsurfing job.

I met Sam Leonard at Leverick Bay, which had just opened in September 1982. I was hired as the beach manager, but only stayed from November through February. During that time, Bert would come in for lunch every day. I wanted to learn how to scuba dive, so Bert said, "Oh, here's a cute young thing, I think I'll take her scuba diving." And the next thing I know he was certifying me, and then I was working for him.

We got married in 1987. Six months later, Bert decided to retire and I started running the business. In 1989, we opened the Pirate's Pub and two years later, I started serving food, not just drinks.

After two hurricanes in 1995 and 1996, I moved back to my condo in Idaho. Amy Thurmond, now a famous artist in the British Virgin Islands, did a terrific job managing the bar. Bert kept asking me to come back and I did for a month in 1996. Then Hurricane Bertha hit and that was it for me. We sold the island within 10 days!

We moved to Florida until the hurricanes started hitting the state. Now we're in California, and just checking to see how the weather is here.

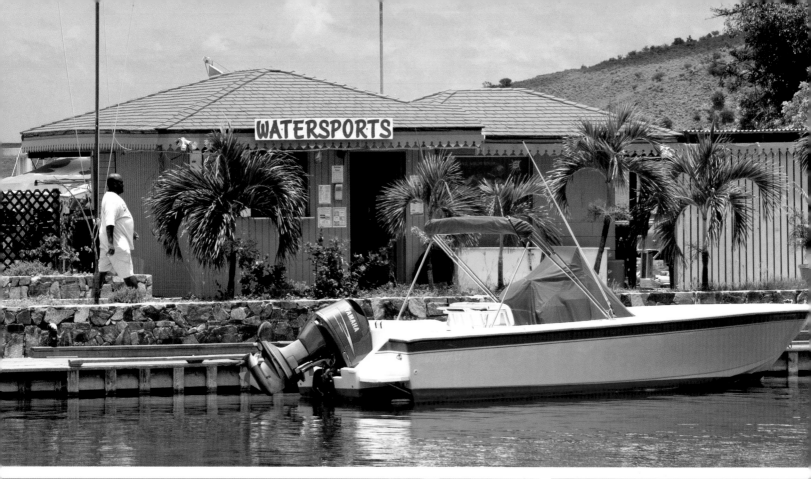

above: Views of Leverick Bay.

Elihu Rhymer:
Educator and Entrepreneur

Early Childhood in North Sound:

I was born in Virgin Gorda on Nov. 27, 1942. I had a lot of fun as a child. Back then we did things kids used to do, not things kids do nowadays. First of all was your duty to your family. My father, a man of great wisdom and character, was a farmer. As a little boy I had to get up very early in the morning and milk the cows. I played, I fished and I did chores. My father got up usually around 3 a.m. and would wake me up at 3:30 a.m. to read passages from the Bible. We grew up in a moral household.

People cared about each other in our North Sound community because we needed each other. For example, when a child got sick and needed treatment in Tortola, where there were medical facilities, the family would wake up a neighbor and ask for help. This meant that the neighbor could very well lose a whole day and night and have to change his schedule, but he did it.

Christmas was great. There used to be a competition for the last boat that would return from St. Thomas just before Christmas. Of course, for most of us it was the first time we would see a toy. We didn't have bicycles and those sorts of things because there were no roads – the roads were just stones. As a matter of fact most of us who got new shoes wouldn't wear them because we didn't want to get them messed up by those stones.

There was a story about a guy who took a walk on Christmas Eve afternoon. He had his shoes strung over his shoulder, which most of us did, because we wanted people to know we had shoes but we didn't want to damage them. So this guy was walking really fast and he hit a rock and cracked his toe. He looked down and said, "Oh, thank God, my new shoes weren't on!"

Working Together to Make a Living:

Back then a lot of people went to St. Thomas to work. The rule was that you could stay for 29 days and then leave, returning for another 29 days. Later on visitors traveled by yachts to the North Sound. As kids we used to get lobsters and sell them to the people who came in the yachts. Can you imagine buying a 2 or 3-pound lobster for 25 cents?

Often two or three people owned and shared a small fishing boat. Larger boats were owned by groups, because nobody had enough money to buy his own boat – so everyone had to cooperate. The community worked together, which was a particularly important part of my childhood. You had to think about the other person, because at some point in time you were going to need that person's help. It was the true quality of village life. Your own behavior was a reflection of your home.

Education in North Sound:

The headmaster at my school was Mr. Bregado Flax, who taught most of the people there to read and write. Before that there really wasn't an established school. My grandmother, who used to have a little school,

helped me a lot. Most people believed that there would be no education after primary school. But I was fortunate enough, thanks to Ralph O'Neal and my father, to continue my education in Tortola and then Antigua for college. Eventually I became headmaster at St. Mary's School in The Valley.

Concerns About Virgin Gorda:

Virgin Gorda is such a lovely place. I was beginning to get the feeling that the community I was trying to describe from my childhood had disappeared – in the same way that the joy and wonderful feeling that one had at Christmas had also disappeared, because people no longer visited each other's homes or spent time together.

It made me realize how progress can change a community and send it reeling, undoing all those wonderful ties that once held people together and created respect for each other. That happened especially after the hotels came in.

On a positive note, we were happy because the hotels brought us better housing and employment – but at the expense of losing some of our connection and reliance on one another. This has changed the character of our community.

Even more distressing was the loss of community leadership that once existed in Virgin Gorda. Politicians seek direct contact with the people in order to preserve and expand their own power base – and so they are doing away with the middlemen who were once the community leaders.

Today, Virgin Gorda is a completely different society with fewer shared commitments. It's more of an individualized society. The Virgin Gorda that I grew up in was a lovely place, even though we drank some sugar and water and ate a piece of bread. I'm not saying one needs to have that again, because I do prefer to drive my little truck or car rather than ride on the back of a donkey. But I do think there were wonderful things we've lost, things that made us more human to each other.

above: Gun Creek views.

North Sound

Positive Influence of the Hotels:

The changes in Virgin Gorda began in the late 1950s and became rampant when Little Dix Bay, Bitter End and Biras Creek were developed. Virgin Gorda was lucky that the original investors like the Rockefellers, Mr. Hokin {Bitter End} and the Norwegian group {Biras Creek} were what I call "philanthropic entrepreneurs." They were businessmen and entrepreneurs, but they were people who were willing to do things that would not necessarily make themselves wealthier. Instead, they wanted to do something positive for others. That was a good time, a transitional period of growth, and these investors were attentive to the people of Virgin Gorda and their needs and concerns.

People were able to send their kids to school beyond primary education and ultimately to university. I believe I was the first person to come over to Tortola for secondary education in 1956. Others followed.

Racism Did Not Exist:

Fortunately, people in Virgin Gorda never understood racism because it wasn't part of our experience. We first saw white people as missionaries, ministers, doctors and later those who traveled to the island in yachts. They were always kind to us, so we didn't experience racism and the kind of resentment that would only be known by those who grew up with it.

I think if the more aggressive entrepreneurs coming here now had first come to Virgin Gorda then it might have been a bit of a shock for most people here. But now I think people have reached a certain level of prosperity and ownership so they really don't have anything to fear. I also notice that people here are integrated and respect each other.

The Need for a Recreational Space:

I want our children to continue to have the kind of fun we used to have. I look at South Sound where we used to go boating and fishing. It was such a pretty place. I'd like to see a beautiful community park there with trees and playgrounds on the beach so that kids and the older people can have a nice recreational place to go.

That is my dream.

John Rhymer: Former Pastry Chef at Little Dix and Owner of the North Sound Superette Store

Early Years:

I was born in Virgin Gorda in 1938. I was schooled, raised and grew up right here on this little island. As a little boy it was quite rough for the kids, but I think it was something we were accustomed to. As a child I knew the name of everybody living on this part of the island, the North Sound. It was the good old days.

I started going to school when I was 5 years old, and the school was located at the area called Gun Creek. It was a big wooden building run by the Methodist Church, which started most of the schools on the British Virgin Islands after slavery. I remember my first teacher, a guy named Bregado Flax. He was one of the first teachers here. Later on Ralph O'Neal came and taught me during my last years at school.

First Jobs:

Kids at that time weren't exposed to too many things, and most of us would follow in

the footsteps of our father and mother. My father fished and traveled to St. Thomas on small boats, so as a young man I started going with him. Then he got a job with the government as a road warden, in charge of cleaning the road. I worked with my dad and that was the first pay I ever made. I was 17. The government paid $1.75 a day. All you were doing was cutting the bush from around the road, throwing the stones out. It wasn't really a road. It was a track.

I started going to St. Thomas for work after that. At that time American immigration laws were very tough. If they caught us staying over the 29 legal days' work, they'd send us home. We had a big boat that belonged to a guy named Robinson O'Neal, a native of Virgin Gorda. The cook on the boat decided to leave. He heard that I could cook, and he sent for me. This was a new experience for me. My interest in cooking came from my mother, a great cook who used to cook for the men of Tortola. I'd worked at a bake shop in St. Thomas for a month and enjoyed it very much. But finding a good job as a chef was all but impossible. So I took the challenge and went out there to cook for 10 men on the boat.

I was in my early 20s when I left the boat. I stopped home to North Sound and met my wife, Sylvia. She's now the pastor of the Church of God Holiness. At the time I was young, born poor but filled with great ambitions. So I built a little house on North Sound. I spent two more years on another boat and then returned. Sylvia and I were married in 1964 just after the opening of Little Dix Bay.

Pastry Chef at Little Dix Bay:

I didn't have a job when I got married. Little Dix's very first chef, Chef Kramer, was looking for a young man who could cook. Venita, a lady from North Sound, took it upon herself to recommend me to the chef. So I got a job, but I needed a place to stay in The Valley.

I remember walking in the kitchen at 2 a.m., and the chef, this tall Canadian man, looked at me and asked me if I knew how to fry an egg and cook bacon and

sausage. I said yes. They had other men cooking there, and I learned from them. I started as a breakfast cook, then line chef and then Little Dix closed down for six months. Chef Kramer went to the manager, pointed his finger at me and said, "You see that man? Don't lose him!" The chef said he saw something good in me. He was a nice man, and he didn't come back to Little Dix, but he sure did me a good deed.

I worked as a cook, and they had a French pastry chef named Alain Boutin. We became good friends. He told the chef that he wanted me to work with him, which we did for about 10 years. Then he started a bakery in The Valley with his wife, Melody.

I learned from Alain, and after he left the manager made me pastry chef. I received formal training at the Culinary Institute in New York. Over the years as more development took place on the island I was sent to other places for additional training. It's a job where you never stop learning. I went to St. John's Caneel Bay, back to the Culinary Institute, Boca Raton, Florida, and Dallas, Texas, before I retired in 2000. We received an award in the Caribbean competition for best pastries. It was the first award Little Dix ever got.

My Store at North Sound:

I started saving my money during my first 10 years at Little Dix Bay. I realized that the North Sound needed a store. You had to go to Tortola if you needed a pot, a glass or a spoon. My store was the first one to open in the North Sound. It's been here for 30 years and it's still going strong.

opposite: John and Pastor Sylvia Rhymer;

above: Views of North and South Sound.

North Sound

above: Clennell Vanterpool at the keyboard;
left: Hammock in Saba Rock's garden;
opposite (clockwise from top left):
Leverick Bay;
Christmas Tree at Little Dix;
Fun at Saba Rock;
Lennox at Biras Creek Bar.

Chapter 5

Chapter Five:
Resorts, Restaurants and Music

Virgin Gorda: The Way we Were, 1960

clockwise from top left: Hauling in construction materials at St. Thomas Bay for Little Dix; View of what is now the Virgin Gorda Yacht Harbour; Construction materials land at St. Thomas Bay. All photos by Euan McFarland, circa 1960.

Chapter 5

Laurance Rockefeller: Founder of Little Dix Bay

Elegant, reserved, understated, and utterly respectful of the natural environment. Such are the hallmarks of the Virgin Islands resorts at Caneel Bay and Little Dix Bay, Rosewood Resorts, and such were the traits of the visionary philanthropist who built them: Laurance S. Rockefeller.   *– David Kirby*

In David Kirby's profile of the "Pioneer of Ecotourism," he explains Rockefeller's respect for the land and its people while producing a gorgeous commercially viable resort.

"Mr. Rockefeller was a pioneer in designing and building low-density, informal buildings, committed to the importance of environmental integrity," said Clayton W. Frye, Jr., a former Rockresorts vice chairman.

During his lifetime, Rockefeller also advised U.S. presidents on this ecological need and received the Congressional Gold Medal in 1991.

Rockefeller, who wasn't afraid of the challenges faced in building in a out-of-the-way place, discovered Caneel Bay while on a sailing trip in 1952. Caneel Bay Resort opened in 1955 and Little Dix Bay opened in 1964 on Rockefeller's "wilderness beach" with 14 "stilt houses." Much has been added since then, but Rosewood Hotels and Resorts, which now manages both resorts, has always attempted to respect the original integrity and vision of the "quiet Rockefeller."

above top: Little Dix Spa;

above below: Little Dix Bay's entrance.

opposite: Little Dix Bay before the resort was constructed (photo by Euan McFarland, circa 1960).

The Honorable Ralph T. O'Neal: Ex-Minister from Virgin Gorda to the Legislative Council of the British Virgin Islands

The Beginning of Little Dix Bay:

We were moving from a peasant society into a commercial-industrial society.

It was a very difficult time for the people, who had been accustomed to "real" life for generations, to adjust now to vehicles and heavy equipment. When Laurance Rockefeller decided to build Little Dix Bay Resort, he brought in a contractor, an architect, and used a big firm from New York, and others from England. His license [with the BVI government] stated that he had to spend one and a half million dollars within five years to produce this development, nothing grand.

This gentleman, McFarland, was appointed as his personal representative, and his job was to keep the peace with the Virgin Gordians and the project. He did a wonderful job! At the time, I was labor commission-er and also the covenant secretary for the Minister of Trade and Production. So I was involved in the project quite a bit.

There was a real emphasis on working with and protecting the Virgin Gordians. Let me give you a few examples. Vehicles couldn't travel faster than 15 miles an hour, because you had old people in the village and farmers walking their cattle to the water, and these people were not accustomed to traffic. One day, a vehicle hit and killed a cow, and the driver was fired. The people complained about the bright lights and the cars in the night when they were going to church.

They did a wonderful job of working with the people, and having meetings with them to keep them abreast of what was happening. This wasn't easy, since Little Dix was going to be down in the bay, using property which was either owned by the Crown or leased to

farmers. Those leases had to be rescinded, and people here had to give up their land for small amounts of money.

One problem was that when we had what was called the "ground sea," Little Dix Bay was used for cargo boats, rather than their regular docking at St. Thomas Bay. It was a problem because the folks at Little Dix, a first-class hotel, did not want to disturb their guests. But the government passed legislation to provide for the boats to have "road right of way" entry to Little Dix Bay when there was a ground sea.

It was a most interesting time. I advised Rockefeller not to introduce legislation for everything, but rather to keep having meetings with the people – discuss with them, talk with them, show them, and let them make the decision. And Rockefeller was so respectful of that process.

In October 1959, we had the final meeting in St. John. Our side was pressing the government side for work to begin, but their representative insisted that the surveying and the investigations be submitted with their reports.

Finally, Mr. Rockefeller stopped all the talking and respectfully said:

"You and your government have been very cooperative. However, I want you to go back to Virgin Gorda and tell the people that work will be started on October 1 this year. Work will be started even if I have to get the men to throw rocks in the sea and then pay them to take them out!"

The representative just sat down on his haunches! I said to myself, "The boss rules!" Work started on October 1, with 50 men employed. They started to work with picks, shovels, and wheelbarrows, doing the roads.

To better understand Mr. Rockefeller, let me tell you about this old man who came to one of the meetings. He said, "Mr. Rockefeller, I have something I would

like to say to you. I'm an old man. The government has requested that I give up my leased land. I am too old to work in construction, too old to be a waiter in the hotel. So, what must I do?"

Mr. Rockefeller said, "Mr. Ammon, I am going to give instructions to the contractor that you will be employed on a weekly basis, you will clean the areas on the lakes and plant trees, and you are not to be disturbed. And a day you don't feel like coming to work, you don't come! Nobody's going to bother you. But you will receive your pay every payday, straight."

And you know, every time Mr. Rockefeller came to Virgin Gorda, he would inquire to me how Mr. Ammon was getting on. And he would find out if they were taking care of him. He did that until he died. And I said it's not all the men who have money who treat folks like that! Many people don't know that about him!

There were many people who represented an "anti-Rockefeller sector," and were upset with what they called Mr. Rockefeller's "spreading his tentacles" over the islands, after he came to build Caneel Bay Resort in St. John. The commissioner here, a man called Howard, who was married to an American, used that fact to get in with Mr. Rockefeller and interest him in coming to the British Virgin Islands. Before he bought the land for the big development, he bought Sandy Cay, near West End Tortola, then Devil's Bay and Spring Bay, two lovely Virgin Gorda beaches, on the condition that they would be turned into national parks. He realized that if he built Little Dix Bay, there would be a need for beaches for other people, so he provided for them. Since then, the government has added The Baths, now a national park. So there was a lot of good that came of it.

opposite: Pastries at Little Dix Bay's New Year's Eve;

above (clockwise from top left): Caroline Whitlock and Rose Gardener; Caswell Pondt's Indian Lamb; Darvin George; Coconut Chef.

Resorts, Restaurants and Music

above: Views at Little Dix Bay;
opposite: Boats at Little Dix Bay's jetty (photo by Euan McFarland, circa 1960).

Martein van Wagenberg:
Managing Director, Little Dix Bay, A Rosewood Resort

I joined Little Dix Bay, A Rosewood Resort, in October 2005 after more than 20 years experience in the hospitality industry and as a seasoned Caribbean hotelier. The previous eight years I spent at Grace Bay Club in Turks and Caicos, developing a young property into an internationally recognized five-star resort.

It was actually a return to Virgin Gorda as in 1995 I had been Food & Beverage Director before Hurricane Hugo cut short my tenure on the island.

Born in The Netherlands, I actually began my career in research: tropical plants and plant diseases before deciding this was not for me! Hotel Management School in Maastricht followed, together with Cornell University in the

US before returning to Europe for experience in top European hotels.

My return to Little Dix Bay signaled a new era. A multi million dollar refurbishment program has led to the 'Rebirth of a Legend' after the completion of four years of renovations. Throughout it all, the priority was given to ensure that the natural beauty, lush landscaping and stunning crescent shaped beach were left untouched.

It is an incredible privilege to have returned to Little Dix Bay and oversee this transformation of a resort with so much history. As most people know, it was founded by Laurence Rockefeller as an environmentally focused resort, and his enthusiasm and love for conservation, wildness preservation and ecology lead the way back in 1964. We very much wanted to continue that philosophy: using design and construction techniques that are better for the environment. In our daily operations we look to use the most effective methods of energy conservation and sustainable initiatives for electricity, water and refrigeration and have an environmentally friendly waste water system to recycle water for irrigation purposes. We are conscious of the human environment and use every opportunity to support local businesses.

Striving to uphold the Rockefeller vision, whilst maintaining a luxury resort and offering the finest service is a challenge but one that I relish, and I am committed.

To make a more positive impact on the natural environment we are looking at coral regeneration for our own reef here in Little Dix Bay and developing a number of land based programs looking at landscaping wand habitats in order to enhance the butterflies, lizards, hummingbirds, kingbirds and others that make their home at Little Dix Bay.

One of the charms that Little Dix Bay offers to its guest is the feeling of returning home. Many loyal guests return year after year and bring several generations of family. For many of the staff it is not unusual to have given 30 years of service, so they have seen a couple coming on honeymoon, then returning with their children and now returning with their children and grandchildren! It is like returning to your extended family, which makes a very special and unique ambience.

With such a loyal and long serving staff in place we recently developed a training opportunity to allow a number to experience their position in one of the different Rosewood Hotels and Resorts, like Mexico, New York and Dallas. This offers a new and different perspective on a job they may have done for many years.

Little Dix Bay has a place in the community here on Virgin Gorda. We have a responsibility to all of our staff and, as the largest employer here on the island, a sense of place. Developing the young people is of great importance and we offer as much as possible the chance to gain work experience, as well as offering the coral reef chats to school children and assisting with hospitality based competitions.

Virgin Gorda truly lives up to its 'Natures Little Secrets' tag line. It is an island of stunning beauty with a hard working and dedicated community, a place where people of all ages can visit and be reminded of a world that is difficult to find nowadays: where there is a sense of community, a place of great beauty and a warm welcome.

Little Dix Bay, A Rosewood Resort is part of Virgin Gorda's history and part of its future.

A Family Affair: The Story of Bitter End

Taken from an article by Dana Hokin, granddaughter of the original owners, Bernice and Myron Hokin, and now owner of Bitter End.

In the summer of 1964, the Hokins sailed into North Sound. They were captivated by the natural beauty, and they returned frequently on their chartered ketch, *Tontine*.

One year they found a shorefront pub with five cottages, called *Bitter End*, owned by Basil Symonette, an eccentric Englishman and yachtsman, built for char-ter captains and adventurous sailors.

During one of their many visits to the Bitter End, Myron said he would like to buy or lease an acre to build a cottage. Bernice wanted to spend more time on the beach. Basil said he would think about it, which he did and then said they could buy "the whole place, but not just an acre".   >>

With a pioneer spirit of adventure, the Hokins became the new owners in 1973, and their charter captain became the innkeeper. None of them had ever run a hotel.

With their grandchildren they explored the islands from Anegada to the Dogs. Their family outings inspire all of the many excursions offered by the Bitter End.

Architect Peter Brill helped design the many buildings and cottages. The entire resort is intended to be organic, comfortable and beautiful. Ecological attention to details are seen in every aspect of life.

While the resort has grown over the years, its main purpose has never changed. The Bitter End is still a family run resort, with the Hokins all participating in its growth and dedicated to the enjoyable vacation of every guest.

Chapter 5

Mikhail Shamkin,
General Manager of the Bitter End

I came in 1971 from Tuscon, Arizona, to Antigua to run a hotel, and I never have gone back. In 1976 I came for the first time to North Sound, sailing in with Don "Squeeky" Street.

Before the Bitter End, I worked in seven or eight Caribbean islands, the last of which was running Prospect Reef and Long Beach in Tortola. How did I come here? It's a good story. Last year Dana Hokin called me and asked if I'd be interested in forming a company, Bitter End International, and running the Bitter End. So, in January, 2006, I became the C.O.O. and Dana is the managing partner. I moved here with my wife Dawn and two children, Sasha and Nikolai, in April of that year.

Here's our philosophy. We are going back to the basics of what the Bitter End is all about. The old management company was striving to develop the proper-ty, making new private villas. We put the cabash to that idea! As the Bitter End is 30 years old, from when it merged with Tradewinds, we realized the need to refurbish the infrastructure, rooms, the Emporium, our Pub, etc.

Myron Hokin's concept was simply that this was a wonderful, extraordinarily special spot and it needed to be appreciated and preserved.

Having worked in so many Caribbean islands, I have been able to learn their unique work ethics. This has been terrifically useful for me here, a melting pot of so many different nations, to know how to motivate people. It is critical to understand people and their culture.

People ask me: "How is to work over there?" And I respond: "Picture working inside a postcard!" What a wonderful life!

Jan Oudendijk: Formerly Interim General Manager of Biras Creek Resort

Coming to Virgin Gorda:

I am a newcomer to Virgin Gorda, and I've been here for less than a year. Bert Houwer is a personal friend of mine and he requested that I manage his hotel and advise him on strategic future options for Biras Creek, which Bert purchased some 10 years ago. Basically, Houwer had been managing the hotel from a distance, and wanted to secure its future so his teenage sons could eventually decide what to do with the property. The Michigan-based company, Victor International,

has recently signed a 15 year lease to run Biras Creek, with its new General Manager, Michael Deighton.

History of Biras Creek:

Biras Creek was built by a group of Norwegians in 1973. Houwer, who is Dutch and grew up in Argentina, was vacationing here 10 years ago with his sons when he saw the property up for sale. He thought it was an excellent investment, and a place his

David Brick:
Manager of Saba Rock

Personal Background:

I've been in the Virgin Islands for 20 years now. I spent my first 10 years in St. Thomas, and the last 10 years in the British Virgin Islands. I was a farmer in Illinois, but I got out of it after we experienced some bad years of drought. I kind of came to a crossroads in my life, one I never thought I'd find myself at. It was just one of those start-over situations, and since I was single and free of responsibilities, I asked myself, "Where would I really want to be?"

In the mid-80s, I had friends who'd been on vacation in the U.S. Virgin Islands, so I took a chance. I bought a one-way ticket. I didn't know anybody, I didn't have a job, and I had never been there. I planned to stay there if I liked it, or go someplace else if I didn't. I was certified for diving, knew a bit about sailing, and bartended in college. So I worked in a hotel in the U.S. Virgin Islands, but I always found myself coming to the British Virgin Islands on my days off.

Chapter 5

family loved, especially for the sailing and fishing.

Houwer is very much aware that if you own something in Virgin Gorda, you also need to play a role in the community. He certainly did that three years ago by donating more than $100,000 in computer equipment to the North Sound Primary School. Bert strongly believes in helping the youth of Virgin Gorda learn how to use computers, which is a valuable tool for their future, and a far better way to spend their time than watching TV soaps.

Thoughts About Virgin Gorda and Its Future:

I've been very pleased to see that there are still environments in the Caribbean like the British Virgin Islands that haven't changed much since I first visited the Caribbean in 1969. You don't need locks on the doors. You can keep your keys in the car, because no one will steal your car. This is so rare nowadays in the rest of the world.

I have worked as a foreigner in nine countries. I try to share my vision and experiences with others, never forgetting that I am a guest in this country, which means I need to respect and work with the local people.

right: Views at Biras Creek.

Resorts, Restaurants and Music

I took a shortcut to South Carolina, got married, and ended up staying there for a short period of time. But I didn't like being back in America after being in the islands for 10 years, so I took a job working in Tortola. John McManus, the owner of Saba Rock, offered me this job after his former manager left more than five years ago.

John McManus, Owner of Saba Rock:

The owner, John McManus, is from California and lives in Sausalito most of the time now. His business is really based in Hawaii, where he owns four restaurants, each with its own unique style. It's not a chain.

He used to keep sailboats around this area, and he would come in and sail around here or sail down island, and spend a few months doing that. He got to know the area pretty well and he got to know Bert Kilbride. They were kindred spirits in certain ways, I think. John gave Bert a standing offer – when Bert was ready to move, John would be interested in buying the island. My understanding is that when the hurricanes hit in 1995, Bert had enough. So John made him an offer, and they reached an agreement. It took about a year or so for John to get the permits and complete the plans, so once he got that all done, Bert moved to the States.

John came in, scraped Saba Rock completely down to rock and started over. It took two years to open Saba Rock in 1999.

I'm passionate about gardens. Ours has grass, which you just don't see much in the British Virgin Islands. I'm currently adding an orchid garden, always trying to improve.

The Beauty of North Sound:

The North Sound is a beautiful spot. There's enough to keep visitors occupied for a few days, especially the charter boat people. They'll come up and spend a couple nights here. We have Leverick Bay, the Sand Box, Biras Creek, Bitter End and Saba Rock, so they can hit a couple of different restaurants. It's not crowded, not overdeveloped, and the key to that is the national park here that won't be developed, which will help keep it unspoiled – hopefully throughout my lifetime. That's the key: keeping development under control.

I keep getting further and further away from civilization as I go along, but I think I'm kind of at the end here. Virgin Gorda just has a whole different feel. There's something about it. I'm really very happy here. It's a great spot, and it's got almost everything you'd want in life.

Esther Wheatley:
Owner of the Fat Virgin, North Sound

Early Years:

I was born in Tortola and my parents were from Virgin Gorda. My mother, who passed away, was from the George family from North Sound. My dad, Ralph O'Neal, was from Spanish Town, or The Valley

In Tortola, we spent most of our vacations, summer, Christmas and Easter, here on Virgin Gorda, splitting our time between the two families. At that time, the two villages weren't connected by a road, so you had to travel by boat or walk the trail.

It was a simpler time, an easier time, a gentler time, I think. People were more laid back than they are today. There weren't too many "Non-Belongers," so everybody knew each other and seemed to interact a little more than they do now. People looked out for others. On Sundays, we would go to church, and then have a nice lunch at home. Then, in the afternoon, we'd do something called "walking out" and walk from house to house and greet families and say hello. It was really wonderful.

Education:

I went to school in Tortola until I was about 11, and then I was sent to boarding school in Barbados. I attended college in Brooklyn, New York, and then Parsons School of Design. But I always came home. I always knew I would come back. Even when I dated, I always checked out my companion's British Virgin Islands' potential. Would this person be able to fit in my life? So I had to come home.

I met Vincent Wheatley in 1991, after I returned home to work. Fate, what can I tell you! After being abroad, you never really imagine that you'll come home and find someone. It was a nice surprise. We've been married 15 years, and I think he's the perfect match for me because we share the same love for Virgin Gorda. We want the same things and we really like the lifestyle. We're totally content with life here.   >>

Bringing Up Kids in Virgin Gorda:

We have two daughters. They're great girls and we're just so happy that we're bringing them up here. They'll have a lot of choices. What's important about Virgin Gorda? Safety. Things have certainly been brought to the forefront because of TV, the media, and what happens to children. So you're well aware of it. But we believe that it's a little safer here and you don't have to worry as much as if you lived someplace else. Why? Because people will still look out for your children.

We have an educational system here that is designed for the average student. It's not designed for brilliance and it's not designed for people who need help. And there's absolutely nothing wrong with that. Students now have a chance to go to college in the British Virgin Islands, which is free for Islanders. They can also choose to go to America or England to study, so I think that it's probably better for our daughters to stay here close to home for high school.

My Life Now:

I came to Virgin Gorda to work in fashion. I ran the store at Leverick Bay, and I left to run the shops at Little Dix Bay. The owner of Biras Creek gave me the opportunity to open the Biras Creek Gift Shop. He said, "It will be yours and all the financial responsibility will be yours, too." It was an opportunity, a challenge that I knew shouldn't be missed.

Friends told me to open up a coffee shop, a sandwich place. No way, I said. I didn't even like being in the kitchen. Finally, the owner of Biras Creek made an offer that I couldn't refuse. Try it for a year – and I wouldn't lose anything. The Fat Virgin started out as a little coffee shop and sandwich place, and it has bloomed into a cafe that now serves lunch and dinner. We started with Chef Monica as a consultant and she provided the basic recipes for the starting menu. Now, we offer fresh, flavorful creations – Chinese, curries, Caribbean – at a reasonable price. We're trying to bring the flavors of the Caribbean to the Continentals.

Food in Virgin Gorda:

I think we're losing our own identity to burgers, fries and chicken nuggets, and somebody needs to bring it back because our food has always been healthy and nutritious. When I was growing up, we hardly ever ate meat during the week. Meat was a Sunday dish, a special meal. Pea soup was a big meal, and we had lots of fish and fish soup. The women in the North Sound were known for their cooking. Christmas was the best time. We had local specialties, such as guavaberry wine, which is made from pears, and potato pudding.

Most of the time, we had baked Johnny cakes and cocoa for supper. You would take an iron pot, knead the dough, put it in the pot with the lid on, and let it bake and brown. My God! The smell was amazing. Everyone's meal was basically the same, and that's how people ate. It was good.

Don't Change Virgin Gorda:

I just hope that the people who come to Virgin Gorda, who want to be a part of this community, can accept it for what it is and stop changing it. It's not to say that things aren't going to change. Things will change, but you should be able to change them slowly and carefully. If we don't, the things that we love will be lost, and then we'll have nothing.

Paola Moretti Flax:
Owner of Mango Bay and the Rock Café

Coming to Mango Bay:

My dad, from Milan, Italy, discovered Virgin Gorda in 1975. He used to come here with some friends and he fell in love with the British Virgin Islands. Three friends came to Tortola to build three houses together. Then they discovered beautiful Mango Bay, which was much larger than what they wanted, so they decided to add a few more houses, and that's how Mango Bay got started. They bought it between 1984 and 1985, opened it in December 1987, and my husband and I managed it in July 1988. I went back to Milan to have my first child, Carola, and we returned to Virgin Gorda two days after Hurricane Hugo, in 1989.

The beginning was very difficult for me. It was a different world, a nice world, but there were many adjustments to the culture and the language here. At first, I was afraid to answer the phone, for fear I could not understand people when they called me. But everything went well.

In 1995, I met my second husband, Dwite

The Rock Café with Dwite and Paola Flax

Flax, who was born on Virgin Gorda. Dwite's first love was music. He played the saxophone and trained to be a sound technician. He started a trucking company and delivered water to Mango Bay. That's how we met. After my divorce, Dwite and I got married in 1996, and we started a lot of activities together.

We combined both of our passions, restaurants and music, and opened the Rock Café in 1997. We started with an informal sports bar, but we decided that Virgin Gorda attracted people who wanted more peace and quiet, as well as good, quality food and entertainment. So we created what is now the Rock Café, with fine Italian and Caribbean food, and Sam's Piano Bar. And it has really become a popular meeting place.

Next, we turned to Mango Bay, after the original owners didn't want to invest more money in the property. I've been at Mango Bay since the beginning, so my heart was here. Dwite and I decided to buy it a couple of years ago and run it ourselves. So now it's ours. We've been redoing each of the houses, one by one.

Dwite was Sam Leonard's favorite nephew. Chris [Yates] always loved Dwite, and she saw the dedication of his work. Dwite is a lot like his uncle Sam – a leader, someone people trust. People could call him at any time of the night, and he'd jump up and help them. So Chris hired him, gave up all her trucks, and now they work together.

Now, we're developing Pond Bay Estates with Lynn and Fred Hill. All the lots are already sold.

On Being an Interracial Couple:

The people on this island were extremely nice to me when I first came on the island. I didn't have to worry, or even go to the supermarket. They would call and say, "Paola, do you need anything? Did you forget anything?" I wasn't used to this because I came from Milan, a big city where everyone is pretty self-centered. So this was something that made me decide that I would never leave again. You felt safe here and that was very important.

As an interracial couple, it was hard at the beginning. I really think that everybody now deals with me because of me, not because I am a white or an Italian woman, not because I am married to my husband, but because they appreciate me. I feel I have friends who are not only my husband's friends but my friends, too. Our captain, Elton, now accepts us as a team, rather than solely listening and respecting my husband's words. He realizes that when I say something, he has to take it as our words. It's us. So it's good. It's very good.

We've been married nine years and we've been together for 10 years. I'm not saying that the first four years were easy. Dwite fights with his culture and I fight with mine, but it's OK now because we've learned to respect each other and each other's culture.

Once people got used to us, as a couple, being interracial wasn't an issue any more. Actually, people don't consider me white anymore.

Rose (Rosalie) Gardener:
Head of Human Relations, Little Dix Bay.

My Early Days:

My mother, Thelma, who owns Thelma's Hideout, a popular place for folks here on Virgin Gorda, always wanted me to have the best. She worked extremely hard, often in St. Thomas, where foreigners could work for only 29 days, and then had to go off island and return to whatever island they came from. When she could, she'd go back again to St. Thomas.

We were brought up in a strict household, with rules, chores, and good manners. Everything had to be kept in order. If people saw us doing something that we shouldn't be doing, they would speak to us as if they were our parents and make a complaint. I went to St. Mary's, a school run by the Anglican Church. Our headmaster and the visiting priests were also very strict. You had to know your verses by memory, or you'd get lashed. But, reflecting on my upbringing, I'd sit back and smile and thank God for having people like my mom, grandparents, aunts and uncles, and my cousin, Nydia George (Speedy's wife), who was like a sister to me. As I said, we didn't have a lot, but we were brought up in the best possible way. It was such a healthy environment.

Little Dix Experience:

I started at Little Dix Bay in 1960, almost at the very beginning of construction. They opened for business in January 1964. First, I worked as a shop clerk, then in administration, although they wanted me to remain as a salesperson. I wanted to advance, so I trained in banking and worked at the Virgin Islands National Bank from 1973-1976, becoming branch manager and supervisor on Virgin Gorda. I learned a lot. In 1976, I returned to Little Dix, where I had an opportunity to advance. I think I was able to make these changes because I always spoke my mind and wasn't content with staying where I was. After 10 years, I moved to human resources, where my training included going to Cornell University for two summers and visiting different properties that they had at that time. It was a wonderful experience.

I brought many attributes with me when I moved into that department. Since I was already established within my community, my contacts with immigration helped our employees who came from other islands. I worked hard, to the best of my ability, and made sure to give other people a chance. The general manager, Peter Hamill, inspired me and encouraged me to apply for human resources, as did my mother, my cousin Nydia, and my dear husband, Keith, who sadly passed away a year ago.

So here I am today, head of human resources. I work very carefully, and try to walk in other people's shoes to understand them better. Doing that has helped me administer to them more effectively, and truthfully. I believe I'm a better person today because they respect me for who I am, because they know that I am not going to pamper them if things aren't right. I will try to protect them and safeguard them. But if I have to speak out, I am not afraid to do it. I love what I'm doing, very much so.

I Have Seen My Island Grow:

As a kid, we had to walk to school four times a day because there was no transportation: in the morning, lunch, back to school, and during the afternoon. We didn't have electricity until 1970 or 1971. We ate a lot of lobster, fish and conch. My grandmother would plant potatoes and peas. She had property on the upper path of Little Dix, and we'd tend our sheep and our goats. As children, they'd strip us naked and we'd go into the sea and play. These were good days.

Our grandmother and aunts taught us to cook. There was this lady who ran the Virgin Gorda Welfare Club, and all the girls on the island would go there to learn how to sew, make quilts and do embroidery. We studied religion. We had concerts, plays, and no cinema or a park to go to, but we had fun! Everyone improvised with what little we had. We used to have good days. As I said, in those days, our parents were very strict, very strict.

Rose Giacinto:
Owner of Bath & Turtle, Chez Bamboo, and Part Owner of Princess Gardens Development

I came to the island because of my husband, Michael Giacinto. He found this place in the early 1960s, when he had just gotten out of the Marines. He was in the Philippines he became involved in diving. After seeing an article on the British Virgin Islands in Sports Illustrated, he and his ex-wife Fran came down here for their honeymoon and fell in love with the British Virgin Islands. He ran the resort at Marina Cay and later branched out to building and construction.

We met in Dallas, Texas when we both were in the wholesale garment business. My modeling often took me to New York where he lived. Michael and I sort of hooked up, fell in love, and moved to Marina Cay in 1981 after Mike accepted an offer to run the hotel. My family wasn't happy about it. I was giving up whatever I was giving up and moving to God knows where, but it was an adventure and a challenge for me at the time. I was madly in love so I moved. We originally planned to just come down and run the hotel together but things developed over a period of months, and we ended up getting married on Marina Cay in August 1981.

Everybody knew Michael because there were maybe only 50 expatriates when he got here. You couldn't miss him, because he was grandiose and he had this big head of Italian hair. We had a really incredible wedding that lasted over three days, with his brother and his friends joining us in the party.

We lived on Marina Cay for three years, moved back to New York in 1984, and bought the Bath & Turtle in Virgin Gorda in November 1988. It was just a tiny pub, with maybe four or five tables and the bar. The island was growing then with a lot of boat traffic at our marina, and Spanish Town was becoming a destination, because there was no place else. We only had a few tiny restaurants like Chez Michelle, Olde Yard Inn, and Dixie's. We drew a big crowd, since we had a live band, the Entrepreneurs.

Michael expanded the whole area in 1990, with the help of Little Dix, which approached us and said that we needed more space at our little café. So, with our architect and good friend Roger Downing from Tortola, we designed the whole complex of Spanish Town.

Unfortunately, Michael died in July 1992. After he passed away, I could have gone back to New York, but I didn't want to. There wasn't anything for me there. People here helped me. They believed that I could do it on my own. I loved restaurant work and being around people. Basically that's what it's about.

It was hard being a woman on this island, and an expatriate. It took me a few years to get adjusted to the way of life here. It's not the same as the United States. I had to continue on my own and develop the Bath & Turtle. Then I bought Chez Bamboo and expanded the original restaurant. I added outdoor tables, chairs, and a garden that everyone said wouldn't grow in that location.

There are many things I love about Virgin Gorda. It's a small community where everybody knows each other. And I have supportive and loving friends, like Ramona, Speedy, Rudy and Thomas, who helped so much with Chez Bamboo.

Change on Virgin Gorda:

I think that people don't really realize the full impact of what it's going to be like in the next 10 years, with both Speedy's mall and Princess Gardens, which Speedy, the actor Morgan Freeman, my brother Mark and I are developing. In three or four more years, Princess Gardens will have another 17 villas. I am concerned about how Virgin Gorda is going to handle it.

The BVI Investment Club, which is owned by locals, has plans to develop the marina, so there will be a real town here in Spanish Town in the next 10 years.

Every year, you see more cars, more houses, and more people. The population has gone from 2,000 to 3,000 in 18 years. I think that's a lot of people for a little island.

On the other hand, I think the opportunities here are endless, especially for the younger people. Their parents are making more money now. They're able to provide better education for their kids. So it's good to see that. You need to know that the upstanding members of this community had it very tough when they were growing up. So they're trying to provide everything they possibly can for their children, which is a reason why they want to keep their children on the island, unlike the time when most of the older folks had to go off-island to find jobs.

We see new banks coming to Virgin Gorda, and expansion in the government presence here. That's going to provide more jobs, especially for people here, instead of pulling others from someplace else. It makes me happy to see, especially in the summer, school kids who are working in training programs down at the customs office and up at Speedy's.

The children of Virgin Gorda are growing up with great ambitions. They don't want to be waiters in a restaurant. Maybe they might want to own one, or move to upper-echelon jobs. It's hard for me to get good people from here to work in the restaurants, but I think it's good for this community to have new hopes and aspirations.

Chapter 5

Elizabetta and Giorgio Paradisi:
Owners of Giorgio's Table Restaurant at Mahoe Bay

Giorgio Paradisi: In 1992, I moved my family to Virgin Gorda from Milan, Italy, where I was manager of a company. I think our decision to leave Italy was a sort of backlash against the Italian society of the early 1990s. It was the time of "Mani Puliti," or "clean hands," and the company I worked for was experiencing many scandals. I had many problems with them over this, so I was basically disillusioned with the corruption and didn't, like many others, want to have anything to do with it. I was 34 years old and I had options. But I wanted to reject this society.

I have a personal philosophy: The greater the risk one takes, the greater the possibilities and advantages. Perhaps I got that from my parents, who were Southern Italians from a town near Naples. In the 1950s, they moved their family to Milan. Both my father and I made decisions that impacted our families. My father moved his whole family to Milan, and I moved my family to the Caribbean. Both had pros and cons. My children had to start a different type of education and in English, to boot. Moving to another country affects your way of thinking and your identity.

It all happened because of my connection with a close friend, a connection that started with our love of, imagine!, German Shepherd dogs. Both of us started talking about how we wanted to leave Italy and try something new. We had this possibility: a restaurant project in Virgin Gorda. Although I didn't know anything about restaurants, I always felt that a person could succeed in doing anything if he was determined to do so. It was a huge challenge for me, and I liked challenges. It was a change of life. Unfortunately, it was a jump into the unknown, and it wasn't very easy for my wife [Elizabetta] and my two daughters.

Elizabetta Paradisi: I made my choice without having any idea of what we were doing. I think we have confronted our challenges, but it has been very hard. Sara, who is the oldest, went abroad to boarding school at 14 for five years. That has been a huge hardship for us. In the first years, we did not have the money to travel much. So we didn't really see her grow up, since she came home only for Christmas and Easter. Now, the situation is much better. This year, Michaela went to boarding school at 16, and I've been able to visit and spend more time with her.

Giorgio Paradisi: We've been very fortunate with our daughters. Sara is in law school in London. Both are wonderful and successful people.

Elizabetta Paradisi: Yes, they are both doing so well. Both went to The Valley Day School to start off, and then they went to the Cedar School in Tortola. Then, we sent them to Italy to get a classical education, as we had.

Starting a Business as a Foreigner:

Giorgio Paradisi: My friend decided to step out of the project. He just wasn't convinced when confronted with some of the difficulties we were facing – mostly problems with building permits, selling our homes in Italy in order to proceed with building in Virgin Gorda, going over our budget for the building, getting loans, and so on. For the first four or five years, we fought tooth and nail to make it work. We have never been a wealthy family with capital to spare. We were alone, armed only with our hopes and the wish to work hard. We left a very secure life.

One challenge for me has been to adapt to another culture. My wife criticizes me at times for being too tough and so set on demanding others to follow my own standards, when these standards are not culturally normal for Virgin Gordians.

But all in all, things have worked out very well for us. Someone else might have given up and gone home. I'm stubborn. In the last three years, we have finally done so well at Giorgio's Table that our restaurant now boasts excellent wines and cuisine, and we've been able to build a wonderful villa for our family here in Virgin Gorda.

Clinton James:
Chef at Biras Creek Resort

I came from St. Vincent to this island 15 years ago in 1991. When I came, I didn't have a profession, but I loved to cook. I became an apprentice chef at Drake's Anchorage on Mosquito Island. It was an opportunity for me to learn, both from the chef, and from cookbooks. I was constantly looking at cookbooks, studying their pictures, and eventually just using my imagination to create the dishes I prepare.

Virgin Gorda has made me what I am, a chef! And, imagine! I've been at Biras for eight years. I love what I do.

My philosophy? I think you should have a goal, a dream, and never stop until you obtain that goal. My family is still in St. Vincent, so someday, I would like to go back there and start my own restaurant.

Well, someday.

above (clockwise from top left): Grandma's Kitchen in the vicinity of Fischer's Cove; Thelma's Hideout;
Flying Iguana and 'Puck' at the Airport; Olde Yard Village pool and bar.

Morris Mark:
The "Father" of Virgin Gorda Music

Early Years in St. Lucia and Coming to Virgin Gorda:

I came from a town called Vieux Fort in the southern part of St. Lucia. My family was very poor so I had little opportunity to pursue a higher education. In St. Lucia, I started singing and writing during my earliest years in primary school. I developed a love for beautiful words from my school days when we'd stand up and recite long poems with deep and beautiful meanings, like the "Psalm of Life" and "The Charge of the Light Brigade." So I started to write songs.

Then I came here because a friend of mine said he discovered this wonderful place called Little Dix Bay, just when it opened. He knew that I loved music, so he said, "Maybe you could get a job singing here." I'd never gotten paid for singing. It seemed like if you said to someone that you wanted to be a singer, and do this as a means of survival, as work, they'd laugh at you. They would say things like, "Oh, he doesn't want to work, he's lazy!"

Working at Little Dix Bay:

At first, the only work I could get was in the storeroom at Little Dix. Then one day, some guy who was going from table to table and singing at Little Dix lost his job. Somebody asked me, "Why don't you try to get his job, like a strolling minstrel?" So I did that. It was a little extra money. In those days, it was $3 an hour. I quickly learned how to entertain the tourists, and how to please them with popular songs – folk music, Bob Dylan, Pete Seeger, and Harry Belafonte.

I went to the manager and I asked him if he liked what I was doing. He said, "Yes, I think you're a good performer, the people like you." I asked him if he would consider giving me a raise to $10 an hour. He looked at me and said, "I can get somebody from the United States to do this." I gave up that job, and then I started the first band on the island with some local boys that I trained. We called ourselves The Wanderers. Later on, I formed another band, Morris Mark & the Mark Five. Lynn Weekes joined us, and we've always worked terrifically together. And so the music grew and we went on to new opportunities, such as singing at the 1979 Super Bowl in Florida. Our appearance was sponsored by the Tourist Board and Little Dix, which raised the funds for us to go. It was a really big thing.

At times, playing at Little Dix was difficult because most of the guys in my band were from other countries, which the locals did not appreciate. Now, I do steel drums on Mondays, the Spring Bay Picnic, and my solo performance on Thursday nights. I also play at The Rock Café, the Mineshaft and Biras Creek.

My sons, Morris Jr., Martino and Marcus, and my daughter Miriam, have also joined me. Martino sings and plays bass guitar, Marcus plays keyboard and drums, and they now have their own band called Phase II. When I can get her, Miriam comes to sing with me.

Writing Songs:

I'm happy now. I'm doing what I like to do. I sing, I have my guitars, I play them at home and I just love writing songs for the CDs we have produced: "Simply Beautiful" and "Beautiful Day in Paradise," which Harry Hunter asked me to write for a video. The title song has become the theme song for the radio program called "Melee in the Morning." I have to say that the biggest reward for me is to hear the children sing this song. Everywhere I go, little kids in kindergarten who don't know me, who don't know my name, say "Paradise" when they see me. So I feel like Elton John. I feel like a big star in a little place!

The Magic of Virgin Gorda:

I love Virgin Gorda. There's a kind of magic here that we take for granted. I came from a part of St. Lucia which was so nice and easygoing, where people go for strolls at night and aren't bothered. I found the same thing here. And I very quickly realized that true freedom, if there is any such thing called true freedom in this life, is what I've experienced here. For those of us who have lived here for the past 40 years, we have experienced a moment in time that will never be the same again. Yes, Virgin Gorda is changing.

My newest project is my CD, "Say a Prayer for the Children of the World." Music is one of the greatest gifts that anybody can have. You can reach people with beautiful words which can touch you and make you think.

Shereen Flax-Charles:
The "Calypso Monarch"

Singing Career:

I've been singing since I was 9 years old. My mom used to play the organ at church, so music was in my family. I went to college in St. Thomas and took quite a few classes in voice training, although my major was business. I sang with the choir at school, and I started singing with Sam Leonard and Lynn Weekes when I returned to Virgin Gorda. I still play and sing jazz with Lynn Weekes, mostly at Little Dix Bay.

A few years ago, I suggested to Weekes that we write

some calypso, and then have me perform in competitions. In August 2006, I won the title of "Calypso Monarch" for both the British Virgin Islands and Virgin Gorda.

We're doing a lot of other stuff, including jazz, folk and soca. We own a recording studio on Virgin Gorda at Andy's Chateau de Pirate. Actually, my husband, Walter "Lili" Charles, is the brain behind the studio and he works with Martino and Marcus, the sons of

Morris Mark, who is sort of the "father" of Virgin Gordian music. The studio is called ANVA Productions, and it's a combination of Antigua, where Lili came from, and Virgin Gorda, where Marcus and Martino are from. We're a great team.

We're planning to do some more soca – not the fast, jumpy ones, but more moderate pieces. We're also recording another jazz CD with a world beat influence, so we can reach out to others beyond the Caribbean.

Calypso Music As a Way to Influence Change:

Let me tell you a little about the controversial nature of calypso music, which is both social and political commentary. When you sing about national pride and building for success, it can be very controversial. Calypso has changed a lot since Harry Belafonte made it known to the world. Now, in order to capture a wider audience, we're blending calypso with jazz, folk and a little bit of something else.

We have found that often people from far away don't understand our calypso music, and you have to explain to them that you're singing about a political issue that they may not culturally understand. In order to get others to understand calypso, we have to include music from elsewhere that will complement it, so everyone can understand what we're really trying to portray in our music.

Reggae, which was made famous around the world by Bob Marley, is half soca and calypso. Bob Marley sang about what was happening in his country, the victimization, the persecution, and all those things, and that's what calypso does as well.

We're trying to influence change and talk about what's wrong with society through our calypso music. During a radio interview, I was asked, "What do you have to say to the kids?" All of our songs have something to tell the children, the young people. They need to be sure to get a good education, and stay away from drugs and all of the negative things that will send your life on a roller-coaster.

Wherever I go, my husband and my children are always there with me. Some parents have to juggle multiple jobs, and leave their kids at home. These parents need to spend more time with their children, which will help change a lot of negative things in society. That's one of our goals – to set an example and be good role models. We may be singing calypso or jazz, but our children are involved in soccer, music, fishing and all sorts of stuff. You don't have to have a lot of money to take care of your children. They just need to know that they are loved, and that their parents are paying attention to them. So sharing that message is important to us, and our music reflects that. It's not just about going out and singing and making lots of money.

We're trying to make our music more international and appeal to a lot more people. Some musicians have broken through, like Arrow from Montserrat. He has done fantastically well with "Hot, Hot, Hot," which is an international soca anthem. He's sold 20 million copies, but he's the only performer to succeed at that level. All of the hot music comes out of Trinidad and Jamaica, which we consider the big islands, but I think the smaller islands are starting to have an impact.

Virgin Gorda is actually known as "Musical City." Our main goal is to bring music back and let everybody know that we're here, and that we're doing our best to promote the British Virgin Islands through ANVA Productions and continue singing and competing.

Theo "Junior" Stevens: Dockmaster and Musician

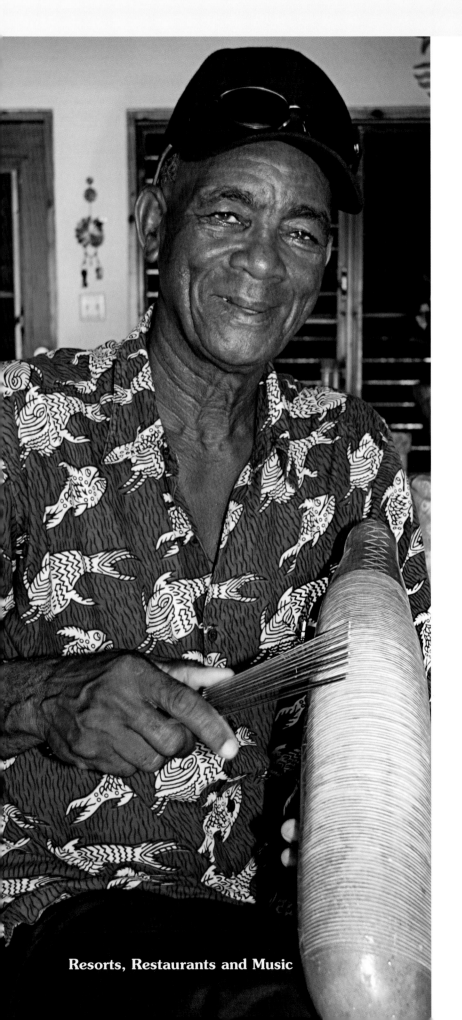

I'm a son of the soil. I was born here, raised here and live here. My dad is from Virgin Gorda, but my mother is from East End Tortola. I have seven brothers and a sister. I've seen a lot of changes here on Virgin Gorda.

Before Laurance Rockefeller came, my dad and others used to raise a lot of cattle in the area that has become Little Dix Bay. We had to work hard, and I was the oldest son, so I had to get up early in the morning and help move the cattle. I helped with most things. Then I had to walk to school up by St. Mary's Church and back, usually four times a day. I loved it. There were lots of things you had to do. Go to school. Go to church every Sunday. Church – that's the way I grew up. I don't drink alcohol, and I don't smoke.

My dad went to St. Thomas with my uncle from East End Tortola. He'd sell cows, sheep, goat, pigs, chickens, potatoes, peas, watermelon, pumpkin and squash. There were no customs. They would leave here in sailboats early in the morning. Sometimes, they went fishing for a couple of months, while my mother stayed behind and took care of me, my brother, and the cows. In those days, there were no roads, no cars, no electricity, and it was OK. There were very few people, mostly families, and everybody treated us well. We had to leave Virgin Gorda to earn money, but we were still hoping for the best back then.

Sailing, Working at Little Dix and Becoming Dockmaster:

As a school boy, I loved the water and I went sailing and fishing with my father and grandfather. I always wanted to be a boat captain, a policeman, or a Methodist preacher. After I left school, I got a job at Little Dix Bay Hotel. Everybody worked for the hotel. Things changed. My dad sold his boat, as did many others, and started to stay home and work at the hotel.

I started off as a carpenter, and later moved to the purchasing department. I worked there for a couple of years and then I decided to head back to the water, where there was a job opening. At that time, Mr. Rockefeller built two boats in the East End of Tortola. There were no yachts in the area at the time, but he built them to take his guests around. I can remember when I went for my interview for a transfer to the Beach House. At the time, Jeff Cook was the manager of the beach house, and he asked what I could do. He said, "OK, we have that boat there. You'll be sailing that boat." It was very windy and the boat was totally different from our local boats. So I told Jeff, "You have to refit this boat. The wind is too strong." He asked me how I was going to refit it. I showed him, and he was impressed. I got the job.

I became the coordinator of the Beach House for the next four years. Things were changing a bit, things were going well. It was getting busy, getting popular at the hotel. But I wanted to go back to sailing.

In 1994, I came here to work as the dockmaster at Government's Dock. I love meeting people. And I also run my own little business. Right now, I'm in the tour business. I have a bus, I take people around in my spare time – on my day off, at dinner time – and I have a boat to take people out.

Love of Music: The Fungi or Scratch Band

My dad was a musician, so I played music from the time I was a little school boy. I came from a family of musicians. My dad bought me a ukulele from St. Thomas. I also play banjo, but I have an instrument made from a gourd, like a squash. Let me tell you how I make it into a musical instrument. You leave it on the vine until it's dry, and then you clean it up and put one or two holes in it to hold it. You get the seeds out, and then when you're ready to decorate it, you get a hacksaw blade, you score it around and then you put whatever design you want on it. To play it, you need an Afro pick to scratch the gourd, to scrape to the beat. It makes wonderful music. Our bands are called Fungi or Scratch bands. They are almost the same, but really, the Fungi bands have electrical instruments and a "gut bucket," which is really a bath pan with a small hole in the center. Then you put in a stick, a piece of wood, 2x2, about 3 to 4 feet. When you play it, it sounds like a bass.

We play now at Little Dix, sometimes twice a week during the high season. People seem to like our Scratch and Fungi music, which really is one of the oldest types of music in these islands.

above (clockwise from top left):
Martino, Lili and Marcus; Morris Mark performs at the Rock Café; Martino, Marcus and Lili's band at Leverick Bay.

Resorts, Restaurants and Music

Elton and Lincoln Sprauve:
The Mineshaft

This was my father's dream. Milford Sprauve. First he wanted to open something down there (indicating the beach area on the Atlantic side), but it was pretty rough down there. So we came up here one day, saw the sunset, and that was that! It was all about him. We decided right then and there to open a place for the folks to drink a pina colada and see the sunset. In 1994 we opened with just snacks and drinks. Now we have a full menu!

Resorts, Restaurants and Music

Chapter Six:
Beauty all Around –
Beaches, Sunsets, Flora and Fauna

Beauty all around

Beauty all around

above: Barracuda flying over the full moon;

opposite: Pond Bay

Beauty all around

above: Savannah Bay;
opposite (clockwise from top): Devil's Bay; Mahoe Bay; "La Dolce Vita" at Mahoe Bay.

Beauty all around

above: Cirrus;
opposite (clockwise from top left):
Hibiscus; Palm leaf; Sea grape bush; Bird of Paradise.

Beauty all around

opposite: Full moon;
above: The Coppermine.

above: Jellyfish;
left: Purple Seafan;
opposite: Turtle at Mahoe Bay.

Chapter 7

Chapter Seven:
Underwater Wonders

opposite (clockwise from top left):
Snorkeling over the wreck of *The Rhone*; School of Permit fish; squid; Yellowtail Damsel;
above: Blue Tang school.

above: Barracuda;
opposite top: Stingray; left: Cow fish; right: turtle.

Chapter Eight:
Change, Progress and Community

The Honorable Ralph T. O'Neal

One day, I was traveling on a boat from Virgin Gorda to Tortola and talking with a fellow passenger. We saw a fellow fishing on the rocks, hoping to get a bite.

My companion said, "What do you see there?" I said, "Well, I see a gentleman there fishing."

"Is that all you see?" he asked. I said yes.

He said, "Well, I see a man struggling for existence."

And the more I think about that phrase, the more I realize what a struggle it was for people in the British Virgin Islands.

When we were little boys, we saw a fellow who used to sail on boats, and we figured he had a good life. Well, some of us tried it, and we thought it was too tough. You can talk with Mr. Elmer George, who for years sailed on boats, and he'll tell you how rough it was.

I hear a lot of people talk about culture, but there are two things that they never mention. An integral part of our life was going to church. Serving God was the first calling in our lives. It was a center of our life: meeting there on Sundays, celebrating Christmas and Easter, listening to concerts and programs. Churches provided education for our children.

We also have a long history, even before slavery was abolished, of being a community that helped one another.

Perhaps the fact that we have moved from being a peasant society into a commercial-industrial society explains why our culture has changed from what I'd call "giving a hand" – helping each other, being available to stop whatever one's doing and helping a friend in need, whether it's building a floor or laying some blocks. You'd arrive to help and there would be some breakfast or drinks and food. Maybe spend two or three hours, say, to help someone pull up his boat out of the water, as there were no mechanical means of getting the boats.

It's sad to say that it's disappearing. But in some cases, one can see why it's not possible to do some of these things. But in other ways, I suppose, perhaps people get lazy. Yet, we still see that spirit of helping in a lot of our people here. For example, when there's a storm brewing, you still see that spirit at work.

opposite top left: Little Dix Bay Captain Malcolm;
opposite right: Samuel O'Neal and Baaba Heru at the Mineshaft;
below left: Bitter End Yacht Club.

Change, Progress and Community

above top left: Full moon atop the tree leaves; right: Allamandas;
above: Sunset at Mahoe Bay.

Author's Last Thoughts

First and foremost, I wish to thank the people who participated in making this book, without whom it would be just a pretty coffee table book, without a soul. Virgin Gorda does indeed have a soul, made up of its people, its beauty, and its rhythm of life and music.

Those interviewed in this book, whether born in the British Virgin Islands and other Caribbean islands, or those who have come here to live, have told their personal stories, often describing great joys and happiness, as well as sharing their concerns about the island and its future. Forty-three years since the opening of Little Dix's doors in 1964 represent a blip in time, and during this short period of Virgin Gorda's history, the island's transformation from the quiet, community-centered fishing life into one of the world's most coveted destinations is striking.

Those born on the island spoke frequently of the good old days when people cared so much about each other and gave a helping hand to those in need. Those were tough days, filled with hard work, little goods and services, but people had each other and enjoyed life. I hope the younger Virgin Gordians will read those remarks of the early years, which contrast sharply with the present, and that they will understand and appreciate more their parents' lives.

Today opportunities abound on the island, including full-employment jobs, strong and beautiful houses, advanced education, paved roads, medical services and an abundance of churches and stores, not to mention the stunning resorts, restaurants and private villas. In addition, television and the Internet now link Virgin Gorda to the world.

The message I often heard was that much has been lost by progress, but even more has been gained. In the earliest of my interviews, with 90-year-old Waldo O'Neal, I asked him about the possible conflict between the locals and those coming to transform Virgin Gorda. He put it bluntly, "Luckily, it's not been like that!"

Paradise, that's Virgin Gorda to most of us, has a positive and negative side, but the former far prevails over the latter, without a doubt. Please go back and read everyone's words, and you will see this clearly.

Finally, I invite you to look at the last picture and read the words of Morris Mark's song, "It's a Beautiful Day in Paradise," a song that has become so popular on the island, probably because it is both beautiful, and right!

Joan Massel Soncini, Ph.D.

April 24, 2007

Morris Markis ¡It's a Beautiful Day in Paradise¡

From the hills of Biras it dawns upon us and spreads across the land.
The morning sun shining down on sparkling silver sand.
The sea gulls fly, the clear blue sky, they almost seem to say,
¡It's a happy feeling to go on living another beautiful day!¡
Oh, It's a beautiful day, such a beautiful day in paradise.
The sun is shining, the children playing.
It's very nice.
Smiling faces, friendly places, living is so free.
Oh, this blessed country is home sweet home for you and me.
From the Coral Reefs of Anegada, beautiful Savannah Bay,
the coves and inlets of nature's secrets pirates used to hide away.
Norman, Peter, Roadtown, Tortola, West End, Jost Van Dyck,
This natural beauty of which there's plenty, and everything's all right.
Oh, It's a beautiful day, such a beautiful day in paradise.
The sun is shining, the children playing.
It's very nice.
Smiling faces, friendly places, living is so free.
Oh, this blessed country is home sweet home for you and me.